HOW TO KEEP ON KEEPIN' ON

A MOTHER'S GUIDE TO FINDING PEACE WHEN ADDICTION HITS HOME

BY LYNN C. HOTALING

How to Keep on Keepin' On: A Mother's Guide to Finding Peace When Addiction Hits Home

©2020 by Lynn C. Hotaling. All rights reserved.

Printed in the United States of America.

Published by Author Academy Elite
PO Box 43, Powel, OH 43035
www.AuthorAcademyElite.com

Identifiers;
LCCN: 2020900107
ISBN: 978-1-64746-106-5 (paperback)
ISBN: 978-1-64746-107-2 (hardback)
ISBN: 978-1-64746-108-9 (ebook)

Available in paperback, hardback, and ebook.

For Charles, with all of my love
Thank you for the lessons and the blessings.

*"One moment can change a day, one day can change
a life, and one life can change the world."*
Buddha

TABLE OF CONTENTS

This book was written for all the mothers who have been there, for those who are going through it, and for those who pray it doesn't happen to them.

May this book bring you strength, comfort, guidance, empowerment, and most of all, peace.

I send you all love and light, and pray for your family's recovery.

PREFACE

REMEMBER TO BREATHE

I didn't want to let go of him. I hugged him like I might not ever see him again. That's how it felt. I honestly didn't know if or when I would hug my son again. I watched him walk all alone to the security gate. I held my breath as the first security officer stopped him. I had no idea what she was saying to him, but I knew by the way I was trembling that it probably wasn't small talk. I watched as he moved on to the next guard.

Unbeknownst to Dylan, the first security officer was watching him intently. I couldn't help noticing as she stared my son up and down while she described him on her radio to notify the security guards up ahead.

What could she possibly be telling them? What was she suspicious of? Who am I kidding? Here it was, Christmas Eve, and a young man is boarding a plane after saying a tearful goodbye to his parents and siblings. And, did I mention, he was high as a kite and looked like he'd been run over by a truck?

I watched as he walked through the line and waited his turn. Tall, blonde, handsome, yes. But also emaciated, ashen, and scared to death of what was to come. I was so intent on watching him, I didn't notice that the security guard who had stopped to talk to him was now standing beside me.

"Are you with him?"

I didn't even turn around. I was annoyed that she was disrupting my last sight of him in the minutes before he got on that plane.

"He's my son," I answered, somewhat defensively, I admit, hoping that would be enough to appease her. I wanted her to leave me alone to watch him go.

No such luck.

"What's going on?" she asked me.

What? Why was she asking me this? I felt my heart skip a beat, and I froze. There was no way I could tell her what was going on. In a split second, I had formed a lie in my mind and was prepared to give her some story about him going to visit family for the holidays. But for some reason that I am still not quite sure of, as I opened my mouth to offer her this trivial excuse, I turned to look at her, and I stopped. In an instant, I knew I could trust this woman. This stranger I'd never laid eyes on, who, moments ago, seemed to be giving my son a hard time at security, and appeared to be the only potential obstacle in this well laid plan—something told me to *trust* her.

"He's going to rehab," I admitted to her.

"Is he high?" she asked.

"No, I don't think so," I countered, knowing full well he was high.

"I think he's high." Was her reply followed by, "What's he using? Heroin?"

How the hell did she guess that? That's when the fear set in. Suddenly I was extremely hot standing there in the freezing temperatures of the northeast in late December. My heart was pounding. My mind was racing. I was already fighting back the tears, and if she didn't let him on the plane, I knew that would be the last straw. I would crumble, right there, on the floor, in front of the security guard whom I knew, somehow, I could confide in.

"Please," I said. "He has to get on that plane. They're waiting for him in San Francisco."

I repeated, "He has to get on the plane."

I was ready to plead and cry, whatever it would take to ensure he was on that plane when it took off. This literally was a do or die situation. If he stayed here, I didn't know if he would survive. I silently prayed, *don't let him die. Put him on the plane.*

That's when the security officer said to me "He's going to be alright. We'll get him on the plane."

I looked at her, startled, because I was prepared to hear the worst. *He can't be allowed on the plane, he's a drug addict, he's high, he's a risk, etc.* She must have seen the look on my face and, of course, coupled with the fact that I was speechless and stood there just staring at her, she looked me in the eyes and added softly, "He can't come back. We'll get him to California. But he can't come back here after rehab to the same friends, the same places, and the same drugs. He'll die here. Don't let him come back."

Okay, so this is when I realized that this woman beside me was no "stranger." I knew at that moment she had been sent to me with a very specific message. Why did I know this? Not only had his doctor and counselor stressed the same warning to me, but so had a very intuitive friend who had spent time with Dylan just a week before. She had, with utter sadness, conveyed to me what she felt surrounding him. "He has to get out of here. Get him to rehab. If he stays here, he will die."

You can imagine my disbelief when this *stranger* at the airport gave me nearly the exact same message. You can tell me I'm crazy for believing in communication from the universe, but I know better. I know as sure as I'm writing these words this was a very clear message I was meant to hear. A message to a mom fighting for her son's life.

The security officer turned to go back to her station, but looked at me one last time and said, "Remember to breathe."

So, I thanked her, the universe's messenger, as she walked away. I felt intense gratitude for her. Not just for allowing my son on the plane, thus saving his life, but for offering me kindness. While some people might very well have been disgusted by the sight of a strung-out heroin addict, she offered only kindness, compassion, and reassurance.

It may seem like a trivial experience, an insignificant incident to some, but I will be forever grateful for this angel at the airport. Not only was this the beginning of Dylan's road to recovery, but, just as significantly, it was also my own awakening to the kindness and goodness in people. This was my first lesson in learning to let go of the pretense and secrets surrounding addiction in my family.

INTRODUCTION

So many wishes streamed through me at the beginning of this journey. I wish someone had told me and that I was more prepared. I wish I knew more about addiction, and I knew how to help him. I wish I'd acted sooner. I wish I could take his pain away. I wish I'd known what I was in for. The wishes just kept coming.

Babies don't come with manuals, and even if they did, there would not be a chapter entitled "What to do when your child becomes a heroin addict."

Until I found myself in that situation, I hadn't planned for such a scenario. Who does? I used to dream about my babies growing up, what they would look like, what their profession would be, who they would fall in love with, how they would surely change the world. Funny though, not once did it occur to me that addiction could strike and totally sideline every hope and dream I had for one of my children.

As painful as this particular journey has been for Dylan and our family, he *has* changed the world as it turns out. His addiction changed his world, my world, his family's world, and, I'd like to believe, everyone's world who knows him, cares about him, and has watched his journey over the years.

There's no doubt in my mind that many people have learned from my son's heroin addiction. It's opened the eyes of people who blissfully trotted through life thinking addiction is someone else's problem. It's caused people to talk, to think, and, I hope, have genuine conversations with their own loved ones about heroin addiction. I'm confident my son will continue to change lives, change minds, and change the world of addiction in his own quiet way throughout his recovery and for many years to come.

You see, as evil as this predator *addiction* is, I refuse to let it win. I refuse to believe there's no lesson in my son's journey. Through many sleepless nights and heart-wrenching days, I searched for the positive in all of it. I looked for the upside of it, prayed for the answer to it, and sought the guidance to learn from it.

Almost a year after that first goodbye when he was headed off to San Francisco, Dylan and I shared another airport trip. It was 4 a.m., and this time, he was returning to rehab after a particularly difficult relapse. The beauty of the autumn pre-dawn hours, in contrast to the direness of the moment, was not lost on me. My heart was full of hope much as the sky was full of luminous stars.

Dylan and I talked about the wonderful workings of the universe. "I feel like there's a bigger picture to this, Dylan," I told him. "I think this relapse happened for a reason. Maybe its purpose is to get you back to the West Coast where you are meant to be, for now at least. Or maybe the lesson you're supposed to get just isn't finished yet."

He agreed. He said, "You know, I've been thinking about that, too, why this is happening again. I think it's all happening the way it's supposed to."

The memory of that early morning conversation with my son will always stay in my heart. Just a mom and her son trying to stay positive through something so difficult and putting their faith in the greater universe.

No mother wishes this life for her child. No mother thinks, *I hope one day my child will grow up to be a drug addict.* But it's a reality that exists. It's a possibility we should realize. It's a matter we should know more about, and it is definitely an experience we should prepare to face "just in case."

We love our children from the moment we lay eyes on them. And that love only grows as we watch every milestone, every smile, every tear they shed, and every accomplishment they master. Watching Dylan learn to dance when he was a blonde-locked toddler is a memory that still brings a smile to my face. Every night after dinner, we would put music on and watch Dylan and his sister, Sierra, spin and giggle, wiggle, and shake. Dylan loved music. And he adored his older sister. Together they laughed and shimmied until they fell down with exhaustion. My heart was so full.

No drug addiction or awful decision or ugly lie can diminish the love a mother has for her child. We might not like his negative actions, but we love our child. That's exactly why there exists nothing in this grand world that will stand in a mother's way of protecting or saving her child from the throes of addiction. It's called 'unconditional love' for a good reason. Just as addiction knows no boundaries, neither does a mother's love.

I knew from the beginning addiction had entered our lives for a reason. Maybe for more than one reason. I knew there was a bigger picture, a master plan in the works. Still, many days and nights it was a struggle to keep this in mind, and the knowledge brought me no comfort. But as the days went by and events turned more painful, I began to learn. Yes, I learned more than I ever wanted to know about heroin, addiction, withdrawals, and all that goes along with the world of drug use, but I learned much more than that. I learned compassion. I learned empathy. I learned patience. I learned appreciation. I learned gratitude. And I learned what is most important in life and what holds no importance at all.

LEARNING TO LEARN

Throughout all of it, I learned to *learn*. I was sure there was a lesson in all of it for me, so I paid attention. I listened to the universe. I listened to the lessons. I looked inward. And I started to change. Prayer, meditation, positive affirmations became a new way of life for me. Perhaps these were my 'coping strategies' at the time. Maybe I was grasping for anything that might bring the slightest indication of peace to my life. No matter how or why these wonderful strategies came to me, they changed my life forever.

Giving thanks for everything in my life became my normal. I began and ended each day with mantras to the universe: Thank you for this day ahead. Thank you for my warm bed, my family, my house, my job. Thank you for my health. Thank you for the love of my children.

Thank you for the hugs, my coffee, the sunshine. Thank you for not taking my son from me today. Everything, big and small, seemed worthy of my gratitude.

Daily meditation became a vital and joyfully anticipated routine. Focusing on repetitive positive affirmations became my new practice. All of this changed the way I viewed the world, the way I coped with my son's addiction, and the way I felt inside.

Slowly, over time, things became clearer for me. It felt as if the clouds and doom began to lift, and the realization gradually dawned that life is very wonderful. With all its trials, tribulations, lessons, and blessings, life is an amazing gift. There's much to learn and even more to be grateful for along this journey.

As I sit here today, I can appreciate that Dylan's journey with addiction was the catalyst that opened not only my eyes but, more significantly, my heart. There have been many more lessons for him along the way which he has met with strength and confidence. But that's for him to share with you one day.

For now, my gift to you is this book. Within its pages, I have shared stories of challenge, defeat, and, ultimately, triumph. I also share many of the prayers and affirmations that have helped me to find peace, comfort, and positive change over the years, and still do. Use them as you see fit, make them your own. My hope is that you, too, will start to feel the light begin to shine again.

DISCLAIMER

This book is offered as many things, but what it's *not* is another book about the war on drugs, the evil effects of drugs, or a story to scare potential drug users straight. It's a story about my son, Dylan, a heroin addict. *(Hence my decision to use "he/him" for consistency as I refer to our addicted children throughout the book.)*

This is a story to let every single mother of daughters and sons, mothers perhaps like you, who are going through a similar journey, know that you are not the only one. I want to help you understand that the things we go through, the things we feel and say and do when we have a child who is an addict are normal.

Although no two addicts are exactly alike, and no two moms are precisely the same, many of the stories in this book will, no doubt, strike a chord with moms of heroin addicts. We all share enough in common—a child who is a drug addict—to be able to relate to the events, feelings, emotions, fears, and situations described in the following pages.

I hope what I have written will resonate with mothers of addicts everywhere. My goal is to bring you some comfort. This is written to let you know that, although there are days you feel very lonely and think you must be the only mother in the world feeling the pain of an addicted child, you are truly not alone.

Although we think we are all "experts" on addiction once we have lived it with our own child, this book is not meant to take the place of professional advice. It's humbly written from a place of compassion and love for those parents living with an addicted child so you know: peace is possible.

CHAPTER 1
DENIAL—NOT MY KID

*It isn't the mountains ahead that wear
you out, it's the pebble in your shoe.*

—*Muhammad Ali*

I don't even remember driving the 20-plus miles to reach him, but I know I made it in record time. The phone call had come, "Your son's been in an accident," and my adrenaline took over. Too scared to imagine what I would find when I arrived, I focused on the road in front of me and prayed.

After dropping out for a while, Dylan had recently returned to college. In order to live at home, he'd chosen to make the 140-mile roundtrip commute four days per week. I knew he was stressed out between his class workload and the early morning drives. I had seen the signs. I noticed the changes. But he assured me he was "okay," so, I ignored what my gut was trying to tell me.

Dylan was on his way home from class when the accident happened. I pulled up to the scene, jumped out of my car, and ran towards the wreck. His car was on its side and smashed up pretty badly. My heart pounded as my mind prayed, *please let him be alive.* I saw the policemen, the firemen, and then I spotted Dylan. The surge of relief almost made my knees buckle as I grabbed and hugged him and cried tears of gratitude in front of the gathering crowd.

He was alive but shaken up. He had fallen asleep and hit another vehicle, flipping his car. A passerby had stopped to pull Dylan from the wreck. Fortunately, no one was badly hurt.

I think I knew even then I was in denial. He "fell asleep." I pretended to accept it, but in reality, I believe he was high and had nodded off behind the wheel. At the time, I pushed the thoughts from my mind. I was just so grateful he was alive, and I didn't want to dwell on it so I acted as if everything was okay focusing on the fact that I still had my son to hug. Sadly, I continued living this lie for quite some time.

It's been said many times, the three most dangerous words in the English language are **not my kid**. No mother wants to believe her child is using drugs, let alone heroin. It's far too painful for any of us to wrap our heads around. No one ever warns us before we give birth of the chance our child will grow up to be an addict. We dream of our babies growing up to be many things...an addict is not one of them.

Parents aren't the only ones in denial. Most addicts are too, at least in the beginning. Sometimes, the denial stage never ends. They're unable or unwilling to see the problem and they will minimize it, justify it, excuse it, and even ignore it. They will deny the impacts of their drug use. Maybe it's just too painful to admit they're slowly killing themselves, or they may see addiction as a failure or a weakness. Perhaps it's too hard for them to recognize the havoc they are wreaking on themselves and the ones they love. Maybe they're just too far in the throes of their addiction to even contemplate the issue. The bottom line is they don't see the problem, and until they do the problem doesn't change.

Growing up, Dylan was a beautiful, tow-headed boy who loved to ride bikes, go-karts, and mini-bikes. He enjoyed fishing and hiking, and camping out under the stars. He loved to spend time with his friends but even more time with his family. He didn't like to stray too far from home, coming in every day after school and sitting down at the kitchen table to start his homework while he talked my ear off about the day's happenings. He loved to swim and kayak, and he was a terrific catcher on his baseball team. He even enjoyed a good game of football. Oh, and did I mention he had an incredible sense of humor? He made everyone laugh with his quick wit and subtle jokes. He was always handsome, smart, kind-hearted, and caring. He loved his family and enjoyed every minute of his summer vacations to the Cape, his trip to Disney World, and his visit to Costa Rica. He lived life. He enjoyed life. He laughed. He loved. He didn't pretend to be anyone but himself. He didn't try to be cool. He didn't try to be a superstar. He was just Dylan. A typical, happy, down to earth kid. And everyone who met him quickly took a special liking to him.

He graduated from the D.A.R.E. program in fifth grade and could recite all the reasons why "drugs are stupid." He took the oath with all his little 11-year-old friends not to do drugs. He was sure, as sure as an 11-year-old can be, that drugs and alcohol would play no part in his exciting future to come.

So, when he tried smoking marijuana for the first time in 8th grade, I reminded him of his oath. "Drugs are stupid; people using drugs are dumb; I'll never do drugs." His words from not so long ago.

And then I reminded him again in 10th grade when he was foolish enough to bring marijuana to school where he got caught with it, and expelled, and thrown off the baseball team.

Okay, 8th grade, let's chalk that up to adolescent experimentation, maybe. Fast forward to 10th grade and I'm thinking, *that's genuinely stupid,* and I was pissed. My thoughts tumbled over themselves and demanded to be heard. "This is where it stops. Fun time is over. No more smoking weed. Done. Over." To reinforce this, just in case I wasn't being taken seriously, I mandated drug counseling once a week. He obliged. He also pretended he was done smoking marijuana. And I pretended to believe him.

WHEN REALITY AND DENIAL CLASH

By 12th grade, Dylan was smoking marijuana daily. Before school, after school, before baseball practice, after practice, before bed, and again when he woke up in the morning. Every chance I got, I lectured him and threw out his stash when I found it. I yelled, threatened, explained, doled out consequences, and I pleaded.

"Stop. You're screwing up your life and your future. You're too young. You're killing brain cells, not to mention your motivation. You'll go to jail if you're caught. You won't get a job when you can't pass the drug test." And on and on my laundry list of reasons and scare tactics went, falling on deaf ears. He was 18, and he was going to do what he wanted to do. So, we continued to do battle regularly over his rebellious ways.

Dylan graduated from high school and was accepted to the college of his choice. But then August came and went, and he didn't. Being the home-body and family-oriented guy he always was, he decided not to go away to college but to stay home and attend the community college. Okay, we'll eat the college deposit. It's fine. At least he's going to attend college. And he did, for a while.

When the last of his childhood friends left to attend residential colleges, the change in Dylan became clearer every day. Since staying behind, he became more of a loner. He became withdrawn and quiet keeping to himself. He stayed in his room a lot, and I made excuses for him. I pretended everything was okay, and kept hoping for the best.

One day, he walked into the kitchen, and I saw him as if for the first time. Who was this boy? He was skeletally thin, with his tee shirt and jeans hanging off him. "Don't you have class now?" I asked. He told me it was cancelled for the day. That was the third cancellation in a month, and I wasn't buying it any more. "You're cutting class. You won't pass." He shrugged and left the room.

His moods followed him outside the family circle, and he began arguing more frequently with his girlfriend. On more than one occasion I was drawn to his room by loud shrieks and bangs as the two of them physically attacked each other and destroyed his bedroom. His pupils were pinpoints, his face was drawn. His personality had done a complete 180.

Something was going on, and I couldn't just blame it on marijuana anymore.

Searching his room, his book bag, and his pants pockets, I discovered pills. Mind you, I had no clue what I was looking at, but thank the universe for the almighty internet. All I needed to do was put in the shape, color, and code on the pills. I had my answer.

Depending on the day, my son was using various forms of painkillers, including but not limited to, Percocet, Oxycontin, Hydrocodone. Common theme here…opioids. A chat with his girlfriend confirmed all I needed to know, but wished I didn't have to hear. He had been abusing opiates for quite some time. She told me, "I can't believe he hasn't overdosed yet." Words that chilled my blood.

Ever the mom, I went into fix-it mode. I drove straight to the restaurant where he worked nights making pizzas, and pulled him out the back door.

"This is where it stops. You're going to get help. Tomorrow, I'm taking you to the doctor. You'll do whatever he tells you to do. This crap stops here. You're done with the drugs. Understand?"

My son was kind enough not to debate reality with me and agreed he needed help.

The next day, as planned, we met with his doctor. I had the privilege of hearing my son tearfully explain his drug history to Dr. Lennon. How long, how often, how many. With all the sordid details spinning in my head, I had all I could do not to fall off my chair.

It should not have come as a surprise when I was confronted with, "Your son is addicted to drugs." But, I'm a mom. And, like most loving moms, I was so profoundly unprepared that I went into shock. I just wasn't ready to hear those words. But there it was. Out in the open. The ugly truth. I have a son who is an addict.

The one thought that kept replaying in my mind? *No mother should ever have to hear those words.* Followed by: *I should have protected him from this. How could I let this happen to my son?*

When I went home that night, I explained the news to my husband. Maybe he was as shaken as I was by this revelation, but he certainly didn't show it. In fact, he had no comforting words, no emotion, no visceral response to this blow to our family. In hindsight, I probably knew then that I was about to ride this journey without his support or comfort. He was going to deal with the facts in his own calm way while I prepared to deal with the flood of emotions pulsing through me.

NOTHING IS EVER THE SAME AGAIN

So, the journey began. The one that would bind Dylan and I more closely than ever, closer than we ever thought we could be. The journey would bring us to tears, to outrage, and eventually to our knees. We had no clue how long the road would be or what hell it would lead us to. But there was no turning back. Without even consciously realizing it or saying it aloud, we had each committed to see this through.

Life is funny that way. Everything seems to be moving along swimmingly one day, and then BAM! You're blindsided with words such as, "Your son is a drug addict." You hadn't planned it, hadn't expected it, and certainly weren't prepared for it. But you're a mom, and you'll handle it.

So, I told myself, *no more pretending it's not really happening. No more thinking tomorrow will be magically different. No more acting as if everything is fine.* Brave thoughts. But the path was long, and little did I realize, we were just beginning. I thought my head was out of the sand, but there's always more sand.

Dylan was prescribed Suboxone to help him with the cravings for opiates. He saw his counselor and his doctor frequently. He had an appetite, was gaining weight, and had found his beautiful smile again. He even re-enrolled in college. He seemed to be off to a great start to recovery. Naïve mom thought everything was flowing along steadily once again. But what I was about to learn was, when relapse knocks, the addict is still home.

Fast forward a few years. If I thought hearing, "Your son is a drug addict" wasn't quite unbearable enough, the universe just wants to make sure you get the message, so it punches you in the gut with "Your son is a heroin addict" for good measure.

Who the hell is ready for that one? Heroin didn't even exist in my world growing up. I didn't know anyone who used heroin. WHY would anyone use heroin? This was a complete curve ball thrown at me, one that I did not even see coming. But here I was faced, once again, with the ugly truth. Dylan had a weakness for opiates, and the journey was to be continued.

It took Dylan a few years and a couple of half-hearted attempts at rehab before he was able to admit to himself that his problem with drugs was destroying his life. When he was ready, he made the decision on his own to get serious about his recovery.

After several months of being clean and sober, my son actually admitted to me that it had made him angry when I would walk past him pretending not to notice that he was high. That's right. The addict was in denial, but he was pissed off when he realized his mother was, too!

We can't kid ourselves. Parents are as expert at the denial technique as their addicted children. We deny, we downplay, we make excuses, and sometimes we even support their addiction, financially and emotionally, without realizing what we are doing.

We refuse to accept the truth right in front of our own eyes because it's much too painful to address. *My son a heroin addict? Never! That just doesn't happen to people like us. What must that say about me as a mom? It's a phase, kids go through it. He will grow up and stop on his own. It can't be that bad if he still holds a job...* the rationalizing goes on and on. We tell ourselves anything to make the hurt a little more tolerable.

Every day the self-talk of excuses and denial in my head got me through. It helped me deal with the horrific events playing out in front of me. He came to the dinner table, his eyes droopy. He wouldn't look at me, kept his head down, barely spoke. I pretended not to be concerned that he didn't eat enough to sustain a small child. I pushed the thoughts out of my head as I watched him scrape his plate in the garbage and return to his room where he would stay, alone, until it was time to go to work tomorrow and start this charade all over. *He's tired from working all day*, I told myself.

This became our nightly scenario. I told myself, *at least he's showing up for dinner. How bad can it be? Besides, his father didn't bring it up or seem to notice that anything was wrong. Maybe I was worrying for no reason.* We all kept silent about the catastrophe forming in front of us.

DENIAL DOESN'T GIVE UP EASILY

Maybe he had a fight with his girlfriend. He's fine, I would tell myself.

I tried asking, "How was your day?"

In return, he would mumble something like, "Okay. Why?"

He would get defensive, he would be annoyed at any attempt at small talk, and sometimes he would get downright nasty. And yes, on occasion, he could even hurt my feelings, but I made excuses for him. Somehow, I even convinced myself it was probably my fault. *I shouldn't be bugging him. He's a young man; he doesn't need his mother asking him questions.*

One day I was especially worried about his weight loss. I said, with genuine concern,

"Dylan, you've lost so much weight. You don't eat anything. You need to start eating better."

He snapped at me, "I'm fine! What are you so worried about?"

This was not how I was used to being spoken to, and I wanted to cry. But something reminded me, *this isn't Dylan.*

As time passed, things got worse. He would come home very late. Well, at least he was coming home, right? As bad as things were, Dylan would get up every morning and put in a full day's work. His employers admired his work ethic and capabilities. He was so *functional* that it made it even more difficult to accept the truth.

Many nights when he walked into the house, I would think, *where is my beautiful son? Who is this stranger?* He'd lost so much weight that all his clothes hung on him. His soft teenage skin had turned to sores and pimples. His long blonde hair hadn't been washed in weeks. His gorgeous blue eyes were not the same anymore. They were sunken in his head, no sparkle, no life, only pinpoints.

The sad part is, as bad as things were, I would actually go to bed thinking, *tomorrow will be different. Maybe tomorrow it will change.* I tried to convince myself everything would just go back to normal. I never gave up hope. But the extreme fear of what was happening right in front of me numbed me.

I realized much later how scared I really was. And how that fear took over and caused me to freeze in my tracks. It would be easy to judge myself and say *I should have done something sooner.* But looking back, I understand how the vicious cycle of fear and denial wouldn't allow me to do much of anything until I was ready to break the dreadful grip it had on me.

I don't know if Dylan will ever understand that my denial was my own survival tool.

Like him, the addict, until I was *ready*, I couldn't acknowledge the problem that was right in front of my eyes. I had learned many things through my role as mom, and now I needed to learn how to be the mother of an addict. By far, the most difficult and complex vessel I had yet to steer in these ever-changing waters of motherhood. I was trying my best to navigate my way through.

REALITY WINS

As powerful and all-encompassing as denial is, eventually, reality wins. There comes that moment of truth. Strength rises up from depths you don't even realize you possess, and you finally confront the issue at hand. You're ready to meet it head on. No more hiding, no more excuses, no more pretending.

One day, I realized that DENIAL is the enemy. I was finally ready to say, without excuses or rationalizations, "My son is a heroin addict, and he'll die if I don't do something."

The first thing we can do to help our addicted children is to acknowledge the problem exists. Stop pretending before it's too late. We have nothing to be ashamed of. This is life. Embrace it, the good, the bad, and the worst. Maybe, just maybe, if Mom can make the conscious decision to recognize what is actually happening to her child, maybe her child will eventually jump on board as well. Or, maybe it will take him awhile longer. Maybe he's not ready to face it, to address it, or to put his energy into recovery. But we can't do it for him. We can only do this for US.

I can tell you that stepping out of the denial you've been living in is the first gift you can give yourself. You deserve to do this for YOU. You deserve to stop living a lie. You are under tremendous pressure every day, and pretending, stressing, worrying, and making excuses only increases that pressure. It's time to let that shit go. Until you do, you won't begin to heal. You won't be who you are meant to be. You're stronger than you think, and yes, you will be able to handle what comes next.

WORDS HAVE POWER

The first step is recognizing what the problem is. Say it out loud…**My child is a heroin addict.** Plain and (far from) simple, it's the raw truth. He's still your child, and you're still his mother. And the universe will bring you everything you need to handle this journey. Just do your part. Show up, acknowledge it, and ask for the courage and strength to get through it.

When the time came that I had to admit to myself what was happening, that my son was dying in front of my eyes, and I was pretending it would just go away, I was devastated, lost, and in despair. I needed help almost as desperately as my son did.

His own father wasn't acknowledging the problem. When I tried to talk to him about it, the conversation went nowhere. It was evident to me that I couldn't turn to him for answers. I was very much alone. Somehow, I knew I had to reach out to my higher power. That's when I made the decision to start each day with a prayer to the universe. Before my feet hit the floor every morning, I would pray for the strength and guidance I knew would be necessary to get me through another day.

Although this flowing river of addiction took me through many phases and many different emotions, my prayers became my habit and my comfort. I learned to pray and meditate on what I felt I needed on any particular day.

Somehow, the universe was always accommodating in bringing me what I needed. I was given strength when I needed it most. I was brought guidance from unknown sources. And I was granted comfort on days I thought there would be no relief from the fear and constant worry.

If not for addiction in my family, I don't know that I would have ever appreciated the gracious energy of prayer. I'm grateful beyond words that I was given the great fortune of experiencing the capacity of this universe to alter my life and emotions. You owe it to yourself to recognize this power in your own life.

Whatever, whoever your higher power is, I encourage you to give it a try. Whether you call him or her God, Buddha, Jehovah, Allah, Jah, aliens, the universal soul, or Mr. Man in the Moon, it doesn't matter. We all have someone or something higher than ourselves, and it's imperative that we reach out to that entity when we feel powerless. Take it from me, right now is one of those times.

I can't stress how strongly I believe in the power of these requests, prayers, appeals, pleas, petitions, mantras, meditations, and affirmations—whatever you choose to categorize them as. You'll find one at the end of every chapter in this book. These are just some of the daily prayers I used along my own journey. Feel free to change the words so they feel right for you personally. Focus on each one when you feel the time is right in your life (you will know!).

Don't just take my word for it, and please don't discount it as nonsense. See for yourself. You'll receive what you're focusing on and what you're asking for. They work. And you deserve to feel them work for you.

From all I have come to understand, I believe through positive statements, affirmations, prayers, and mantras, you can change the way your brain thinks, what you believe at your core, and thus the way you present to the world and to yourself.

Take this first step in the direction of being YOU. You have a hard journey in front of you. You need to be the best you. Once you begin to walk in your truth, you'll notice that things have a way of unfolding more clearly in front of you, and you'll be more available, more present to deal with the events taking place.

*I ask you for the strength and courage
to recognize the truth in front of me.
Please give me the power to stop making excuses
and accept this reality without pretense.
Allow me to acknowledge my child's addiction
so that I may walk in my truth
and be the best me I can be.
I ask this for my highest and greatest good.
And so it is.*

CHAPTER 2
ENABLING & CODEPENDENCY—
RETHINK THOSE GOOD
INTENTIONS

A child is a mother's strength and
a mother's weakness.

—Unknown

So, you're no longer in denial. That's a huge step. You've recognized that your child is an addict. Painful, but true. But did you know most of us mothers of addicts are currently or have at some point enabled our addicted child? We enable an addict when we help him avoid the consequences of his negative behavior. While well-intentioned, our attempts to protect him from his own behaviors are only allowing him to continue his addictive patterns.

Did I enable my son? Hell, yes! However, in my own defense, at the time I didn't even understand what that word meant or how what I was doing might actually be hurting him more. I thought I was helping him when in reality, the only thing I was helping him do was continue his drug use by removing the natural consequences of his behavior.

Enabling is Bad News

I admit, it took me a long time to realize that what I was doing for Dylan was a textbook example of enabling. I can't say I regret it or I apologize for it. I believe it comes with the title of 'mother.' A mother loves her child so powerfully that she will do anything for him. And who are we to judge how much a mother loves her child? How far she will or should go for her child? Eventually, we learn that enabling behavior is not loving, even if it comes from love. It only hurts him. In time, I was able to see this more clearly.

Dylan suffered from social anxiety. He explained it, he defined it, he wore it on his sleeve for all to see, and he used it for all it was worth as an excuse to use drugs. And, for a while, I went along with this charade. It made it more bearable, I suppose, to have an *excuse* for my son being addicted to heroin. He can't handle social situations; he can't be around crowds of people; it's a legitimate disorder. And meanwhile, he would hide behind anxiety and use heroin every chance he could to avoid social situations.

For some time, he also struggled with depression. Most days, when I confronted him about this, he would claim he was not depressed. He'd say, "It's just the drugs making me that way." Here he was telling me the drugs were causing his depression, yet I refused to see it. I insisted he had a depression disorder and this was causing him to use drugs as a means to feel better. 'Self-medicating' as the experts call it.

In all honesty, it was a case of which came first, the chicken or the egg? Or, more aptly, the depression or the drug use? My son was probably being honest when he explained that his drug use was causing his depression. Bottom line, I was enabling him. I was looking for excuses to explain his behavior. In some small, strange way, having a *reason* for his drug use helped *me* bear it. But wasn't the point to help *him*? To do that, I had to face my enabling behavior.

I came home from work about 3:00 one afternoon.

"Can I use your car quick to run to the store?" my son asked.

Every fiber in my being screamed, *NO, NO, NO! Don't give in!*

"Don't be long," was what came out of my mouth. He assured me he would be right back as he hurried out of the house.

It didn't take me long to realize that the blank check I had left on the kitchen table was missing along with my son and my car. I knew immediately where it went and why. My son, the drug addict, needed money for his fix.

As I sat alone at the kitchen table in tears, I pondered the sadness of the situation and wondered (for the 1,000[th] time), *how did we get here?* Just then the phone rang. "Mom, can you call a tow truck? I'm stuck in a snowbank!" It was Dylan, out of breath and slightly shaken up. Suddenly, his wellbeing trumped everything, and I jumped in my husband's car which was in my driveway and drove to him as quickly as I could get there.

Seeing him safe and able to walk around my car, now buried in a valley of snow, relieved my worst fears, but brought with it a new flood of emotions. Mainly, anger. How dare he wreck my car? How dare he scare me like that? How dare he steal money from me for his drugs? All questions I quickly (and loudly) posed to him.

Realizing the accident was going to involve a tow truck and an accident report (i.e. a phone call to the police), once again, Mom the Enabler jumped into high gear. I made a quick decision, no thought necessary. I had to take the blame for the accident. Since Dylan was high, there was no way I could let him take the fall. Not to mention, after all his speeding tickets, he would surely lose his license, and an enabling mom just couldn't let that happen to her first-born son, could she?

I quickly told him, "Take your dad's car home and stay put! I'll wait for the police. I'll fix this like I fix everything else!"

Truth be told, I was screaming it in his face, letting him know with no uncertainty that I was pissed. This wasn't a position I wanted to be put in, and I wasn't the slightest bit okay with the circumstances that had to be dealt with. Dylan appeared to be unbothered by all of it.

He did as he was told and went home, leaving me to wait for the police so I could give an accident report, and deal with my anger. Once again, the drug addict was saved from feeling the consequences of his behavior, and I took the blame for the accident, so eager was I to protect him. He screwed up and got off scot-free. **This is classic enabling**.

Looking back on that day, I realized I wasn't really so much angry at my son, the heroin addict. I was angry at myself. Angry that I had allowed myself to become such an enabler in my son's addiction. Angry that although I knew it came from a place of deep love and wanting to *fix* everything for my child, I was only helping him to continue to kill himself with drugs.

I also understand now that part of my rushing in to protect Dylan was selfish. I worried that people would find out he was using drugs. The secret would be out. If I took responsibility for his actions, no one would know, and I didn't have to face reality quite yet.

It's not easy to admit we enable our child's addiction, but believe me, I have learned through it all, I'm not the first mother to love her son so much that she tried to 'make everything okay' and lessen his burden while he struggled with his demons. It's what comes naturally to moms.

I've read many books and research articles and self-help manuals that describe enabling. I understand all too well how it works and why. I've studied the process more times than I care to remember. I get it. Although enabling comes from love and fear, it isn't helping anyone.

We don't enable because we want to cause more harm. We don't do it because we're stupid or ignorant. We don't do it out of malice. We enable because we love our children more than life itself, and we would do anything to save them from more hurt and suffering. We do it to spare them just a little pain. We do it because we, as mothers, know better than anyone how bad our children are hurting already from their addiction. We know better than any book can explain the hell our children are going through. We enable because if we can lessen their load, their hurt, their struggles, their pain, through just one circumstance, we'll do it. We do it because we are struggling ourselves. We're grasping at any opportunity to stop further suffering for our child. We can't take the bullet of addiction for them, so we're willing to take any other bullets that come their way. The hard truth is we do all the wrong things with the right intentions.

So, we give him another chance. We make up excuses, we take the blame for the car accident, we call in sick to work for him, we pay the bills when he spends his last dime on drugs, we tell little white lies to the other family members to explain his behavior, and we outright lie when we deem it necessary to 'protect' him from himself. We do all of these things because we are mothers who love our children. But all of this only prolongs the agony and puts off the inevitable.

CODEPENDENCY

Parents of addicts also need to understand the concept of *codependency*. Again, this idea took me awhile to wrap my head around. *I'm not using drugs, I'm not dependent, what are they talking about?*

Codependency is basically a dysfunctional yet well intentioned relationship where a person enables another person's addiction. When we allow our drug addicted child's behaviors to affect our lives to the point where we put their needs before our own; when we can't say no to them even when our gut tells us we should; when we continuously try to control their behavior because we think we can fix it for them… we are codependent.

My first thought when confronted with this term was, *another label that comes with being a mom of an addict.* And, again, I struggled to understand it and deal with it. Eventually I came to understand that the behaviors aren't advantageous to either person in a codependent relationship.

My codependency was just my way of trying to make this situation hurt a little less for everyone involved. My head knew all along how serious Dylan's addiction was but my heart just wanted to protect him. But it wasn't just him I was protecting.

I covered for Dylan countless times when he screwed up. I continuously made excuses for his bad behavior. And, I even went so far as to keep many of his drug-related secrets from his own father in the beginning. I knew how much his addiction was hurting *me*, and I wanted to spare my family that hurt. I rationalized: *I can help Dylan get better without everyone knowing how bad he really is.* I justified it by believing: *His family is better off not knowing the ugly details.* And I reasoned: *This is going to pass. Dylan will stop using drugs.*

I wasn't only protecting the addict from the impact of his drug use I was also shielding the family. So, I made excuses or I just kept quiet. All along telling myself it was best for everyone. Not only was I trying to be the peacekeeper, I was also trying to be the rock. It made me feel like I was doing something positive to calm this storm of negativity we were all living in.

Yes, I was codependent, and I needed a wakeup call. I can recall the moment but not the exact precipitant that caused me to confront the issue. Maybe I had just had enough and finally realized my enabling needed to stop.

I hugged Dylan tight, and I put him on notice. As I looked him in his eyes, I explained that "my enabling behavior stops now. No more making excuses or covering your bills. No more fixing situations, accepting your lies, or pretending you're not a drug addict." I also reminded him, "This is *your* journey, Dylan. I can't walk it for you. *You* have to do this. I love you, and I'll support your path to recovery, but I can't help you kill yourself anymore."

He didn't debate it with me. He understood and hugged me before he walked away. I think somewhere deep inside both of us we knew the *mom* in me probably couldn't stop enabling **just like that**. But we could appreciate that things were beginning to change.

DETACH WITH LOVE

Here's what I know:

❖ No apology is required for loving your child.

❖ Don't beat yourself up for making decisions out of love.

❖ And certainly, don't feel badly for caring deeply for your child who is an addict.

But there will come a time when you have to accept the fact that **enabling an addict is not helping**. As difficult as it is to admit, and even more difficult to follow through with, we have to stop making excuses and taking the blame for them. Until they experience the suffering their addiction is causing themselves and those they love, they may never find their path to recovery.

I wish I could give you a fool-proof, tried and true method to stop enabling your child.

Unfortunately, I don't believe there is such a thing. I don't think there's only one specific way to change our behavior. You have to find it within you. You have to take a step back from the situation and look at things more objectively. Yes, that's a very difficult thing to do when your son is a heroin addict.

The only way to help your child is to let go. "Detach with love" the experts say. Stop trying to control this out-of-control situation because in reality, the addict is going to do exactly what he wants anyway.

Remind yourself:

❖ Say "no" when your gut tells you not to give in to his every need.

❖ Start putting your own needs first.

❖ Don't take on his burdens.

❖ You didn't cause your child's addiction, and you can't fix it for him.

❖ Set boundaries that allow you to love and support your child yet don't require you to accept his behaviors or try to control them.

❖ Let him fall, let him feel the results of his addiction, and reap the consequences of his actions.

All you can do is stand by and watch him and let him know you love him unconditionally. Remind yourself, *enabling him is not helping him.*

Sometimes addicts have to fall on their own. If we moms are always there to catch them, how are they going to feel the "low" of addiction, the repercussions of their actions, the impacts of their behaviors? Isn't that how young children learn? Once they experience the consequences of a behavior, they are empowered.

They learn not to repeat that behavior. I don't mean to make it sound easy. It's not. But as moms, we have to learn to set some limits with our addicted children. *"Healthy Boundaries"* is the term used to explain to us that we need to step back, draw the line, let go, stop enabling. Once you can convince yourself, and trust me, it took me years, you will be able to let go with love.

SAY IT: IT'S FOR HIS OWN GOOD

Here are some specific things you can say, with love, to your addicted child:

- ❖ "No drugs or alcohol are allowed around me or in the house."

- ❖ "If you're arrested, I will not bail you out or pay for a lawyer to defend you."

- ❖ "Please do not insult or ridicule me."

- ❖ "I will not give you any more money— whether it's to pay a bill, buy you food, or put gas in your vehicle."

- ❖ "I will not lie or 'cover' for you anymore— regardless of the circumstances."

Remember: detaching is not abandonment. Be careful not to mix these up, even if your addicted child accuses you of abandoning him. You are not. Nor are you blaming him or judging his journey. You're simply not taking on your child's issues any longer. And that's nothing to feel guilty about. Remind yourself, this is *his* journey, not yours. You're actually doing what is best for him.

Not only will you allow him to feel the consequences of his actions which just might help him begin to make a change, but you're also providing him the opportunity to actually do the right thing and take pride in doing it all on his own. Fly or fall, he has the right to take ownership over all of it. What you can do is be there to support, love, and encourage him on his path to getting well again.

I came across this piece of wisdom on Facebook presumably written by an addict. It's a powerful appeal to all enablers to end our well-intentioned yet misguided efforts. As I read it for the first time, I remembered how many times Dylan had said to me, "You can't do this for me, Mom; you can't fix this for me." I heard him, but I wasn't listening.

LET ME FALL ALL BY MYSELF

If you love me let me fall all by myself. Don't try to spread a net out to catch me. Don't throw a pillow under my ass to cushion the pain so I don't have to feel it. Don't stand in the place I'm going to land so that you can break the fall allowing yourself to get hurt instead of me.

Let me fall as far down as my addiction is going to take me, let me walk the valley alone all by myself, let me reach the bottom of the pit. Trust that there is a bottom there somewhere even if you can't see it. The sooner you stop saving me from myself, stop rescuing me, trying to fix my broken-ness, trying to understand me to a fault, enabling me ... The sooner you allow me to feel the loss and consequences, the burden of my addiction on my shoulders and not yours ... the sooner I will arrive ... and on time ... just right where I need to be ... me, alone, all by myself in the rubble of the lifestyle I lead ... Resist the urge to pull me out because that will only put me back at square one ... If I am allowed to stay at the bottom and live there for a while ... I am free to get sick of it on my own, free to begin to want out, free to look for a way out, and free to plan how I will climb back up to the top.

In the beginning as I start to climb out, I just might slide back down, but don't worry I might have to hit bottom a couple more times before I make it out safe and sound. Don't you see? Don't you know? You can't do this for me. I have to do it for myself, but if you are always breaking the fall, how am I ever supposed to feel the pain that is part of the driving force behind wanting to get well. It is my burden to carry, not yours.

I know you love me and that you mean well and a lot of what you do is because you don't know what to do and you act from your heart not from knowledge of what is best for me. But if you truly love me, let me go my own way, make my own choices, be they bad or good.

Don't clip my wings before I can learn to fly. Nudge me out of your safety net, trust the process, and pray for me, that one day I will not only fly, but maybe even soar.

--Passion (The author's real identity is unknown.)

*Please guide my words and my actions
to do what is best for my child.
Help me to understand how to best support him
without enabling him
and allow him to be held accountable
for his actions and his choices.
I ask you for the strength to set boundaries
and let go with love.
Please remind me to trust the process
and feel at peace.
I ask this for my highest and greatest good.
And so it is.*

CHAPTER 3
SECRECY—DON'T
TALK ABOUT IT

Anything that's human is mentionable.
Anything mentionable is manageable.

—*Fred Rogers*

There has been a lot of research done on addicted families and the *unspoken rules* that exist including the rule, "Don't talk about it" which extends far beyond family. The shroud of secrecy spans much, much farther than most of us realize.

First of all, as I've mentioned, there's this underlying belief that maybe, just maybe, if we don't acknowledge it, if we don't accept it willingly, if we don't talk about it, it isn't true. Maybe if we're good at pushing it away, we can pretend it isn't happening.

No such luck. We already know that's just our denial talking.

Still we try to hide it from everyone. We're in shock that our child is a drug addict.

We're embarrassed. We make it about **us**. *What will the neighbors think? His old teachers? What if my boss hears about it or my coworkers? Everyone will think badly of him. Everyone in the community must be talking about him behind our backs. People might think I'm a bad parent or I did something terribly wrong for him to turn to drugs.*

Such thoughts went through my head for a long time. Too long. I spent far too many months, probably years if I am perfectly honest, pretending that everything was fine. I smiled; I laughed; I behaved as if I wasn't hurting and terrified inside. I acted like my world wasn't falling apart. I talked about my son as if everything were perfect in his life, and he were the same happy child he was when he was a little boy.

I hid the fact that I barely slept. I pretended I wasn't constantly worried and preoccupied with horrible thoughts of losing my son. I went to work and no one ever would have guessed the secret I was keeping. I spent time with friends and never let on that anything was seriously wrong with one of my children. No one knew that Dylan was dying from a horrible, painful disease.

I hid it from everyone. And I hid it well (or so I thought).

First and foremost, I kept this secret from my own family. I worked very hard at keeping Dylan's brothers and sisters in the dark. They didn't need to know their big brother was a heroin addict. I was scared to death they would think less of him. I didn't want them to stop looking up to him. I wanted to pretend he was the same fun-loving, hilarious guy they knew and loved. More than that though, I wanted to protect them. I didn't want them worrying about him. I didn't want them to feel scared. Yes, I just wanted to pretend everything was okay. So, I kept the secret. I figured it was easier that way.

IT'S NOT ABOUT YOU

Believe me when I tell you… I was wrong. The only person I was fooling was myself. In hindsight, I realize everyone already knew. They heard the rumors. They saw the signs. They noticed the changes in my son. It didn't take a rocket scientist to figure out he was a drug addict.

And his siblings? I didn't give them nearly the credit they deserved. Who was I kidding? I raised these children. I knew what intelligent and perceptive people they were. There was no hiding secrets from this family. I had to realize this was not about me. It was about my son, Dylan, who was struggling, and we all had to start speaking the truth.

His siblings watched Dylan transform from a strong, handsome, funny guy to the thin, disheveled, cranky shell of a person. They still loved and cared about him and were worried. They saw me crying even when I thought no one noticed. They sensed the distance between their parents. They knew their mom was not herself. They noticed my thoughts were often elsewhere. They knew I was preoccupied with worry and stressed more often than not. They didn't have all the details, but they knew enough to surmise something was very wrong.

Because they were in the dark, they were even more scared. What was happening to Dylan? Of course they would think the worst. No one was talking to them about the "problem," whatever that was exactly. They were left to their own imaginations. They were too afraid to ask questions and sensed they should just keep quiet and out of sight. They tried their best not to add any more stress to the family and went about their day wondering how it would all end.

They kept the secret, too, without even being asked. They didn't talk to anyone about what was going on with their brother, and they pretended everything was okay. To this day, I can't even imagine what went through their young minds and how desperately they wanted answers. I realized only after the fact how this was impacting their young lives.

LETTING THE CURTAIN OF SECRECY FALL

Once I made the decision to stop pretending, everything changed for my family. There was no significant, earth-shattering event that caused me to change my attitude towards Dylan's addiction. Nothing in particular that made me drop the pretense. Over time, I was literally just worn down. I just didn't have the energy to continue the façade. I felt too tired and overwrought to even care anymore about what anyone else thought. My son was my only concern. I had no time or even the desire to pretend everything was okay. It was far from okay. I was watching Dylan kill himself with drugs, and I actually cared what the neighbors thought? How ridiculous!

Even though it didn't take a catastrophic event to wake me up to this realization, it did pretty much happen overnight. I woke up one day knowing what was most important. And I can tell you, what people thought or said about Dylan or my mothering skills were nowhere on my short list of priorities. Suddenly I didn't care who said what, who thought this or that, who knew, who didn't know.

All at once, I was hyper-aware of the blessings in my life. I was incredibly grateful, especially for my children. Although things seemed pretty grim, I was grateful Dylan was alive. It wasn't too late. I was grateful I had the presence of mind to keep an eye on him until he was ready for recovery. I knew my family was blessed in many, many ways, and I wasn't taking it for granted. And I wasn't keeping Dylan's struggle a secret any longer either.

I was done hurting because some of the local folks were judging my family and watching my son fall from the "perfect pedestal" we had supposedly placed our children on. It was suddenly very clear to me. My children didn't always make "perfect" decisions but the choices they made were always in line with their personal journeys. Everything happens as it's supposed to happen. And in everything there is a lesson and a stepping stone to the next event they're meant to experience. As difficult as it was for me to watch, and even harder for him to traverse, I knew Dylan was walking his own path. I never said my kids were perfect. But in retrospect, I now understand that everything God made is pretty damn perfect.

It was around this same time the lightbulb went off, that "aha" moment when I realized, *I need to talk to the kids, they need to know what's happening.* That's exactly what I did. I discussed his addiction openly with his older sister and younger brothers. It was very difficult because, again, who is ever really prepared for this conversation?

I tried to keep it simple. As simple as addiction can be I guess. "Dylan has a problem with drugs. He's battling addiction to opiates. He's not himself. We're hoping he will decide to get help, but we can't force him. When he's ready, he will get treatment and be healthy again."

Jensen, who is four years younger than Dylan, admitted, "Yeah, I've noticed the change in him. I knew it wasn't just weed anymore." He told me he'd heard the rumors that his brother had been using pills. He was genuinely hurting for Dylan.

Sierra, the eldest, was very upset. "Make him go to rehab! Tell him he has to go!" She didn't understand yet how an addict has to *want* treatment. She felt the urgency of the situation and knew Dylan needed treatment for his drug problem. She was scared, which made her want to see things move fast. She didn't understand the countless times we spoke to Dylan about treatment and how each time he refused because he just wasn't ready.

Trey stayed fairly quiet. As the youngest of the brothers, he was more disappointed that he "is always the last to know." He was too young at the time to totally comprehend what was transpiring, but he wanted to feel like he was part of the solution, and I explained to him that he absolutely could be.

Sage, being very young at the time, wasn't present for this family discussion. She played nearby with her father. By this point in the game, I had already decided that I was going to *handle* this on my own since his father continued to ignore Dylan's addiction. Whether he was in his own denial or it was just his own way of dealing with the stress didn't matter to me anymore. He wasn't helping me, so I was on my own.

I asked all of the kids to be patient and understanding with Dylan. I did the best I could to explain to them that he needed their support, not their anger. He needed their love, not their resentment. I explained, "Drugs change a person. This isn't the Dylan we used to know. But it's still the Dylan we love, even if we don't like what is happening right now. He will eventually choose to get healthy again."

Unfortunately, I also had to remind them to lock away anything valuable because "a person using drugs doesn't think clearly. If he feels desperate, he will take whatever he can find." As hard as it was to watch their faces, so full of uncertainty and fear, I also saw their love. It is hard enough for adults to wrap our heads around addiction; it was going to take time for the kids to understand and work through it.

Believe me, that was one thing I finally did right throughout this whole experience. I explained the problem as I knew it, I answered their questions, I settled their worry just a little, and most importantly, I let them know that their brother needed and deserved their love and support more than ever before. It didn't take much convincing as they only felt compassion and love for their brother. This was no surprise as I knew who they were as individuals. I knew their hearts were pure and sincere when it came to their family.

THE TRUTH EMPOWERS US ALL

Now that my family was empowered with an understanding of the facts, they could also become part of the solution. They were able to finally lend support on the family team—not only to their brother whom they loved so deeply, but to each other and even to me and their dad whom they recognized were hurting beyond words. Letting go of the secrecy gave them the strength they needed to pick their heads up, wrap their hearts and arms around their family, and fight alongside each other for the brother they desperately wanted back.

I had no doubt I had done the right thing. They were part of this family, and they deserved to be treated with respect and dignity. They deserved to know the truth and be treated as the warm, loving, compassionate people they are. They immediately rose to the occasion and became a force to be reckoned with. Not to say they weren't still worried about Dylan and probably somewhat annoyed with the circumstances. They had every right to be concerned.

It was a very serious situation. I also had to respect their feelings of frustration and irritation.

Addiction was new territory for all of us. We were each doing our best to understand and navigate the storm. But it was obvious they wouldn't allow anything or anyone, even addiction, to harm their brother. They showered him with love and support from that day on. Nothing would stop them from helping him beat his demons.

Around this same time, I received a phone call from Jensen's middle school. He had been removed from P.E. class for fighting. Fighting? He was the "gentle giant" everyone knew and loved. Why would he fight? It didn't make any sense.

Apparently, one of the students made a derogatory comment about his older brother the *drug addict*, and Jensen just wasn't taking that.

Instead of punishing him for this mark on his discipline record, I thanked him. I couldn't condone fighting, but I applauded him for sticking up for his beloved brother. I mention this story as just one example of the lengths these kids would go to in order to surround each other with love and protection. That's what a family does. Don't underestimate the power of a family—yours or anyone else's.

Once the secret was out in the open in our family, it didn't seem so unmanageable. No problem, not even addiction, now seemed insurmountable to us. Although we're far from a perfect family, we have plenty of love amongst us. It seemed now that the pretense was dropped, the excuses, the fake happiness, we could get down to the real issue of helping Dylan recover.

I no longer felt ashamed in public of what people might think I did or didn't do to cause Dylan's addiction. I no longer felt like the community was looking at him like he was the devil incarnate. I no longer allowed myself to feel 'less than' in public. And I certainly didn't allow anyone, community members, family members, co-workers, to look down upon Dylan. He's a human being. A vulnerable, addicted, human being worthy of love and compassion. If other people couldn't empathize with him, shame on them. That was their problem. It no longer concerned me or affected my life.

As a mother, I know we all have the instinct to protect our children. Physically, emotionally, and even socially from the comments, opinions and negative deeds of others. I don't think that will or *should* change. We're moms. We're mother bears. We will protect our young at all costs. But I have learned to pick and choose my battles with the world when it comes to my children.

Knowing how not to give energy and emotion to what others think is a lesson well learned through this process of addiction. I had to take a step back outside of myself to see the bigger picture. Others' opinions had no power to hurt or help him. My number one priority was saving Dylan's life, and these people played no part in his recovery. Whether they approved of him or not, whether they understood or not, whether they judged or not, had no effect on our lives. What was of utmost importance was my son and how we could help him become sober and healthy again.

We want our children to be well-liked, respected, and admired. When life throws a curve ball and words and labels, opinions and accusations start flying, we do what we do best. We hurt for our children, and we protect them. We worry what others will think and say about them. I'm here to tell you, it truly does not matter what people think.

Nothing matters except your child who is addicted to drugs. Not neighbors, not friends, not co-workers. They don't understand what you're going through. In reality, it scares them, too. If it happened to my son, it could happen to theirs. And that scares the hell out of them. So, they talk, they make uneducated comments and guesses, and offer opinions to appease their own fears. Don't let their chatter distract you. It's insignificant.

I have a great friend who reminds me: "Others' opinions of you are none of your business." And guess what? She's right! Don't listen to those other people. Look at the big picture. Those people aren't even **in** the picture. If they aren't there to support your family and your child, *they don't exist.*

Yet I still hold compassion for them because they only speak out of fear and unknowing.

It's easy to judge and speculate when you haven't been there. No truer words have ever been spoken than: "You don't know addiction until you've lived it."

To Sum Up

❖ Let go of the secrecy. Take my word for it, you will feel a sense of relief once you have made up your mind to stop pretending. Face it head-on. Your child is a heroin addict and needs help. It's all that matters.

❖ There is a problem. A critical problem that could kill your child. Nothing is more important.

❖ You're not alone. Your child is not the first to be addicted to drugs, nor, unfortunately, will he be the last.

❖ Focus your attention on your child, not the opinions of others. Pretending everything is okay is not fooling anyone anyway.

What bothers me the most about the secrecy of addiction is: if we as moms have a difficult time talking about our child's addiction and opening up about it...how do we expect our child to admit his addiction and ask for help? And how is society supposed to face it head-on if no one is owning it? Shouldn't we moms be the role model for them? If we refuse to keep the ugly secret, our child may find the strength to come forward with the truth and seek treatment.

Please give me the courage to be honest
about my son's drug addiction.
Show me the words to explain it
and discuss it openly with my family.
I'm grateful to be able to bring
addiction out of the closet and
shed light on it in order to
enlighten others about the disease.
Bless me with the gifts of compassion and patience
for those who speak out of ignorance.
I ask this for my highest and greatest good.
And so it is.

CHAPTER 4
SHAME—HOW TO STOP HIDING

Thousands of candles can be lighted
from a single candle.

—*Buddha*

Shame is probably something we've all felt at one point or another whether we're willing to admit it aloud or not. It's usually the number one reason we pretend everything is okay. In our case—that of the mother of an addict—be sure not to misunderstand the emotion. We aren't ashamed of *our child*. We know better than anyone what a beautiful soul he is. We're ashamed of his actions, his behaviors, the things his addiction causes him to do. Deep down inside we know the truth. The addiction is not your child. When he does something awful—it's the addiction rearing its ugly head.

Still, we feel ashamed that it has come to this point. Our worst fears never let us imagine that our child would turn to drugs. How could we have let this happen? We're embarrassed for him. We're self-conscious around the people who we realize know the truth. They have questions, they have opinions, they have fears, too, that it could be their child next. But nothing is said aloud. You don't want to bring it up because you're ashamed this happened to your family. And others don't want to mention it out of fear of offending you. So, everyone tiptoes around the elephant in the room.

It's torture to feel these emotions because of your child's addiction. We live with the shame every day. And then we feel guilty because we are ashamed.

At one point, Dylan, his counselor, Anna, and I met to discuss the impacts of his drug use on his family. At Anna's urging, Dylan was to list all of the ways he felt his drug use had affected his family members. And then it was my turn. She asked me to describe the impacts of his drug use and (here comes the best part) explain to him *"how he has disappointed me."* I almost fell off my chair. I was startled and somewhat taken back by her choice of words. I could only imagine the guilt that phrase she used made my son feel at that moment.

Maybe I was overreacting, but I shot back rather quickly, "Disappointed? That's not a word I would ever use to describe any of my children! I'm not disappointed in who my son is! I'm proud of who he is in his heart!"

I continued to explain how I felt sad that he has an addiction; sad for him that he's not living his best life. I described my feelings of worry, stress, and fear. I explained that his behaviors upset me and that I could not condone them. But nowhere in my laundry list of emotions pertaining to my son did the word 'disappointment' ever appear.

I realize my reaction was somewhat defensive, and I understand Anna wasn't trying to offend us. I am eternally grateful that she was a catalyst in Dylan's recovery process. And I can now appreciate that sometimes, although everyone involved has his best interests at heart, a professional and a mom of an addict may not always see eye to eye.

This is about the same time I realized, *what the hell am I so ashamed of?* My son is sick with an addiction to drugs, and I'm spending my energy feeling ashamed of his behaviors? This is where it stopped. No longer would I give another thought to feeling shame for the things his addiction caused him to do—or not do. I wasn't letting him off the hook. I wasn't making excuses for him. But I was beginning to realize that shame had no place in his recovery.

A mother truly knows her child's heart. She knows the individual she has raised, and the values she has instilled in him. His addiction doesn't define who he is. How dare I allow anyone to make me feel ashamed for what was taking place in my son's personal journey? From that day on, I never lent another thought to the idea of shame. I refused to give it any power over my son or me. I let go of feeling ashamed because I knew the things he had done (and some of those things were not pretty!) to feed his addiction were not *him*. It was the addict in him.

One of the many things I have learned throughout this process is that an addict will do anything to get his fix. Things he wouldn't have dreamed of doing if not for addiction. An addict will lie, steal your wallet, pawn precious belongings, forge checks, spend his entire savings and last dime on drugs. He will break promises, trust, furniture, and your heart in pursuit of a fix. And yes, he will crash your car, lose his job, and perhaps even opt to live on the streets. Does that sound like the child you raised? Of course not. But do not underestimate the power of the beast that has ahold of that person. The addict your child has become will do all those things and more.

However, I was beginning to understand the distinction between the addict and my son. They occupied the same physical body but they were two totally different spirits. They were not one in the same. The disease did not define him.

YOUR CHILD IS STILL THERE

You know and I know—the child you raised is still in there. Deep down inside, he's still alive, heart and soul. His core values, strengths, and innate goodness are hiding deep inside. He might not remember who he is, but you do. He certainly isn't able to think clearly enough to choose to be that person again. But as moms, we know who we birthed and raised. This stranger we see in front of us is the horrible result of a disease. This stranger is still worthy of our unconditional love and compassion—not our shame.

Don't let him feel unworthy of your love. You can **love the person while hating the addiction.** With luck, hope, and tenacity, that person can realize his addiction doesn't make him who he is.

Through it all, you can:

❖ appreciate who they are without excusing their actions

❖ love them without loving their behaviors. Are they less worthy of love and compassion because they're drug addicts?

❖ refrain from judgment

❖ remind them that they are human beings by reminding them that you love them

❖ tell your child: "I might not like the things you do, but I'll always love the person you are."

I reminded myself often: although we never wished for or chose this life for Dylan, he didn't either.

*I ask you to give me strength to let
go of the shame I have felt
as a mother of an addicted child.
Thank you for helping me to remember
that addiction is a disease,
and it's not my fault, and I can't fix it.
Help me to honor myself today as a
mom as well as my child for
the beautiful human being he is.
Remind me to hold my head up as
an example to other moms so
they too might have the courage to be free of shame.
Please help me to remember that addiction
is not who my son is.
I ask this for my highest and greatest good.
And so it is.*

CHAPTER 5
FEAR—THE CRIPPLING EMOTION

*Use your fear…it can take you to the
place where you store your courage.*

—Amelia Earhart

Lying in bed, eyes wide open to the dark, heart pounding, I tried to find the words and form the sentences in my mind to describe my beautiful son. All the wonderful things about Dylan…how would I fit them all in? *His heart as big as his blue eyes. His caring soul. His dynamic sense of humor. His non-judgmental live-and-let-live attitude. His charismatic ability to cause people to like him the first time they meet him. His dimples when he smiles. The proud way he walks like his grandfather. How he adores his dog, King. The depth of his love for his sisters and brothers.*

It hurts my heart to recall the countless times I drafted my son's eulogy in my head. I had myself convinced it was going to be an inevitable responsibility for me as his mother since no one else knows him as well as I do. I contemplated how I could ever do him justice with words, and how I could possibly make it through such a scenario. There were days I stood in my closet staring at my clothes thinking, *I wonder which dress he would want me to wear to his funeral.* Fear had me in its grip and was wreaking havoc on the mind.

It's a parents' worst nightmare. Lying awake at 2 a.m., waiting for the sound of the car to pull in the driveway. While simultaneously waiting for the phone to ring announcing he's been in an accident or he's in jail, or worse, waiting for the knock on the door for the authorities to tell you he's been found dead from an overdose. Every imaginable repulsive scenario the mind can conceive, fear brings to the surface when your child is a heroin addict. A mom's mind conjures all the *what-ifs,* all the negative outcomes, and every possible consequence to each horrific situation. And we do this because we're moms who are gravely afraid of losing our children. We are numbingly aware that he might not survive tonight. Or tomorrow night.

Nights are the worst. Fear rendered me immobile. Helpless, I would lie in bed afraid to move, afraid to sleep, scared to envision the worst, and terrified to wake up in the morning to find his bed had not been slept in. Composing a eulogy or desperately praying into the darkness. Sometimes I'd fall prey to magical thinking. If only I could lie still enough, he'd make it home safely. If. If, if, if only… Fear has a way of playing sick tricks on the mind.

POWERLESS

As if the emotion of fear is not enough to contend with, it causes its repulsive partner, *powerlessness,* to rear its ugly head. Oh, what a gut-wrenching, mind-consuming feeling that is.

Especially to a mom who is accustomed to controlling everything for her family. We "control" in order to nurture, to teach, and to protect our children. Isn't that what moms do? Being powerless contradicts everything we believe about being a mom.

The reality is that we can't control everything. There are so many things in life that are out of our control. We can't fix everything for our children, including their addiction. Addiction teaches us the three Cs of powerlessness: **we didn't cause it, we can't cure it, we can't control it.** Accepting this lesson isn't always easy though.

The first step of a 12-step program such as AA is to admit powerlessness over your addiction. Well, if we expect the addict to acknowledge being powerless, we moms have to be ready and willing to do the same. I know it goes against everything that has been instilled in us since we were little girls. But powerlessness brings humility which is exactly what is necessary to admit that we aren't in control of the situation.

The fear which led to powerlessness which led me to feeling humble, led me to prayer. It caused me to learn how to pray. Really pray. Not the desperate pleas borne of midnight panic.

Those "prayers" were just me trying to gain some control.

Prayer became the only solution to the feeling of powerlessness. I knew I had no control over my son's behaviors or his decisions, so I prayed, and I prayed hard. I prayed while trying to sleep, I prayed while barely asleep. If I fell asleep, I felt as if I never stopped praying. I prayed when I woke, I prayed in the shower, I prayed while driving, I prayed at work, I prayed all day. It was a constant mantra, *Please, God, keep my son alive, bring him safely home.*

Somehow, I knew someone was listening to my prayers. I knew someone or something greater than myself was looking out for him. I still had the nagging feeling that something dreadful could happen to him, but I found some solace in knowing he had a guardian angel watching over him. How did I know this? I guess it's called *faith.* And, looking back now, if not for my unwavering faith, I don't really know how I would have gotten through the worst days.

You can say, "Well, I'm not a religious person." No one said you had to be. It doesn't really matter whether you feel religious or not, whether you believe in God or not. What's important is that you find the strength to let go of the fear and learn to trust in the universe (or your higher power) that everything is unfolding the way it's supposed to. What's important to realize is that no matter how much worrying you do, it won't change a thing.

Fear of my son dying by overdose or a car accident while high was certainly an everyday emotion for me. No mother wants to see her child die, and I knew all too well the drugs were killing him. But there were other issues that caused fear. Like his drug-induced mood swings. I could never anticipate which personality would walk through the door. I wondered, *will he be high and non-communicative? Will he be coming down off his drugs and just nasty? Will he be sober this time and himself, talkative and joking? Will he be miserable and complaining? Every day brought the uneasiness of anxiety: who was going to show up and how bad would it be?*

I learned quickly that living with an addict is like living with Dr. Jekyll and Mr. Hyde.

There were moments that I caught glimpses of the old Dylan. His personality before the drugs. My heart would swell with happiness, and most of all, hope that these moments would last. But they were fleeting. Too few and way too far between.

It was uncomfortable to be around Dylan most days. I always had the apprehensive feeling of watching what I said or how I responded to him. I learned to carefully choose my words or topic of conversation. I knew all too well that he was easily agitated and could become verbally aggressive if I set him off. And, of course, I realized this was because of the drugs. This was the complete opposite of Dylan's personality prior to his drug use. Nonetheless, my world became paved with eggshells which I consciously attempted to navigate.

Then there's the fear that the drug addict you are living with will steal you blind just to be able to get the drugs he so badly craves. So, a parent learns very quickly: lock it up! Take the car keys, hide the wallets, the jewelry, the spare cash lying around, the checkbook, and anything accessible that might be sold for drug money. The fear of losing everything, of going broke, of having your personal and prized possessions stolen from right under your nose cannot quite be put into words. Unless you've lived with an addict, it's difficult to know that particular type of fear. Suffice it to say, it's a fear no parent should have to learn.

It should be noted, you can cognitively be aware of this fact and go to great lengths to lock up everything you own to keep it *safe* from the addict in the family, but in reality, as my own son explained to me one day, "Where there's a will, there's a way." So, you live with the fear that although you've done your best to protect your belongings from your addicted child, he will still figure out a way to get it if that's what he needs in order to get his next fix.

Not a comforting thought.

FEAR'S MESSAGE

Think of fear as the universe sending you a message: *yes, things are bad, they are very bad, but it's not too late.* As long as you're feeling fear, it's not too late. Your child is still alive to scare the hell out of you.

Fear is a normal part of living with an addict. The emotion is real, and it's warranted.

There's much to be fearful of when your child is a heroin addict. And it's okay to be afraid. It's a sorry emotion to feel when caused by your own child, but it's okay to feel it.

Fear can be dangerous though if ignored. It is unhealthy and can lead to untold health issues, and ultimately solves nothing when left unchecked. So, acknowledge it, feel it, but don't let it win. **Use fear to be smart, not frozen.**

Go ahead, be afraid. Be afraid he will die…because he may. Be afraid he will steal your checkbook… because he probably will. Be afraid he will wreck the car…because he just might. But don't be afraid to act, to do something. Use all those fears to mobilize yourself, to motivate yourself to seek help. Use that fear to keep pushing forward, keep looking for answers, keep trying to get your child the help he needs. **Use your fear and you'll transform it**.

Thank the universe for allowing you to feel the fear. Be grateful for the guidance to admit *we are powerless*. Appreciate the humility necessary to let go of trying to control your son's journey. But most importantly, be thankful for the gift of prayer. These are gifts to yourself to begin your own healing.

*Give me the strength to face each day with
courage and all that it may bring.
Help me to recognize my fear and push through it.
Thank you for helping me to understand that
it's okay to be afraid of the unknown,
and for reminding me the more
I learn and understand,
the better I am equipped to handle what comes.
I am grateful for the strength to face my fears each day
with love, respect, and perseverance.
Continue to guide me.
I ask this for my highest and greatest good.
And so it is.*

CHAPTER 6
BLAME—IT HAS TO BE SOMEONE'S FAULT

No one saves us but ourselves. No one can & no one may. We ourselves must walk the path.

—Buddha

It's natural to want to place blame. The frustration, fear, and anger I felt surrounding Dylan's drug addiction resulted in my blaming everyone and everything around me. *It's probably my fault for not doing enough. It's the friends he hangs out with. It's his girlfriend, I knew she was no good. It's got to be his father's fault for doing nothing. And it's those damn drug dealers, if it wasn't for them...* And the blame went on and on.

In some ways, it satisfied me to place blame. For a while, it served me to have someone to lash out at. I needed to be able to point the finger at someone, something that *must* have caused Dylan's addiction. This blame, of course, only served to help me avoid the real issues in front of me. While I was busy placing blame and pointing fingers and trying desperately to figure out who exactly the culprit was, I was avoiding the real fact that my son was a heroin addict.

For a long while, placing blame served me. It gave me something on which to focus my energy so I didn't have to face the real problem staring me in the face. (There's that denial again.)

The truth was, my son was slowly killing himself with heroin. Did it matter whose fault it was?

While blaming everyone and everything, I was also able to accuse everyone of not doing anything to help my son. *Why wasn't anyone helping him? Why wasn't anybody **doing** anything? He was killing himself and yet no one, not his best friend or even his girlfriend, was doing anything.* They seemed to be standing by watching this happen to Dylan. As much as I begged, cried, and pleaded, his own father did nothing. He barely spoke to his own son. *And why wasn't the counselor doing enough? Clearly she was useless, too!*

POWERLESSNESS ⤏ BLAME

The fact is, we think and say a lot of things out of frustration, fear, and that overwhelming sense of powerlessness. Blaming everyone in our path in a time of crisis may be a natural reaction. Knowing we have no control over our child's drug addiction or his decisions or behaviors is an alarming reality check, especially, as I've already mentioned, for mothers who are used to controlling their child's lives in many other ways as they grow up.

I mean this in a positive way—we control their bedtime, their nutrition, their regular doctor and dentist visits, and so much more. Let's not pretend mothers don't exercise a sense of control over their children while they are growing up. If we didn't, their childhoods would be total chaos.

So, we control things to protect our children and assure they grow up happy and healthy. In the normal course of events, they grow up and separate from us and our control in healthy, affirming ways, by going to college perhaps, or starting a job, moving into their own place. A parent still has influence, and adult children often seek our advice and guidance.

But if they turn to drugs, you lose all control as a mother all at once. You can't stop it, you can't manage their behaviors, and you no longer have influence over their decisions or choices. And they certainly aren't asking our advice any longer. You're helpless and powerless.

For most of us, that's a fairly new concept, and we don't know how to handle it. So, we struggle, and we flounder, and we feel frustrated and lost.

And we place blame. We don't know what else to do. We've already established that we're scared and we're powerless. Maybe if we can blame someone for this grave set of circumstances, we might figure out how to fix it. Or, maybe if we blame others often enough and loudly enough, we might lessen the burden of guilt *we* feel.

I personally chose my own husband as my target for blame. I wasn't exactly sure what he *did*, but I was very clear on what he *didn't* do. He didn't help Dylan with his addiction. He didn't make him stop using drugs. He didn't have the gut-wrenching emotional reaction I had to Dylan's addiction. It must somehow be his fault. Irrational thinking? Sure it was. But he was my closest target, and he incurred my wrath.

In hindsight, maybe he really was as worried and tormented as I was, but because he didn't express it, it became easy for me to blame him. Maybe it helped me lessen my self-blame at the time while I accused him of being responsible for his son's addiction.

And, of course, I blamed the drug dealers. Without them, this wouldn't have happened. It was normal to want to hold them accountable for my son's addiction. One day I had had enough. I was at the end of my rope, and I needed to do *something*. I set out to find some of those drug dealers. I wasn't sure where Dylan was on this particular day, and I was out of my mind with worry. I hopped in my car and set out on a mission to find his dealers.

I drove to every location I could remember hearing about where I thought I might find these people. The more I drove, the angrier I became. I was a mom on a mission. I just wanted to find one of them and unleash my fury! Back roads, alleys, downtown high rises. I went to them all.

And then I got lucky. I stopped at a house where I found two drug dealers, and I walked in there like I was Super Woman. I lost my shit, and it wasn't pretty.

I realized afterwards that this was not my finest hour. It was probably one of the stupidest things I've done in a long time. But I needed to place blame, and I wanted them to know it. I needed to get it off my chest. I must admit, I felt a sense of liberation afterwards.

It didn't change anything of course. These people weren't scared of me. They didn't care how I felt, and my son was still an addict. But this is an example of how far a mom will go to try to save her child from drugs.

Once again, during a frank conversation with Dylan, he enlightened me: "It's not anyone's fault, Mom. These dealers didn't force me to do drugs. They didn't come knocking on my door. It was my choice, Mom. I'm a drug addict. I have no one to blame but myself."

Truth is, there is no "blame" to be placed. There are no fingers to be pointed. You can't blame an addict for his disease. You can't blame anyone. No one forced it to happen. It's no one's fault. Even if it was, what good does blame do?

I had more than one friend or family member say to me, "Well, this was his choice; he did this to himself; he has no one to blame but himself." Easy enough to say if it's not you who is addicted to heroin.

I'm not arguing the fact that Dylan chose to take drugs. He made the decision to try heroin the first time. No one forced him. He has free will. He could have said no, he could have walked away, and on and on the *could haves* go. I get it. However, what I WILL argue is that my son never made a conscious decision to become a heroin addict. No one wakes up one day and says, "You know, it's a good day to become a drug addict." Addiction happens, things spiral out of control, and before anyone realizes, there's an addict fighting to survive just one more day.

No One Wins the Blame Game

So, how will placing blame help the situation? Short answer: it won't. This is the journey your child has been given. This is his life. It's his addiction. Let go of the blame.

For now, what's important to remember is your child is a heroin addict, and your child needs help. Sooner rather than later. Now. While he's still alive. Don't waste precious time placing blame and aiming your anger at others or even at yourself. Use that energy to focus on your child. Your child, the heroin addict, needs help before he dies from his addiction. Let the finger-pointing go. Let the 'blame game' stop. It serves no purpose, and it won't save your child's life. LOVE him, love yourself. Stop blaming yourself, Mom.

*Help me to understand that blaming
others for my child's addiction
is not productive nor is it moving
him closer to recovery.
Please give me the wisdom to use
my energy in positive ways
that are for my child's highest good
instead of placing blame on myself or others.
Allow me to continue to let go of blame
and focus on recovery.
I ask this for my highest and greatest good.
And so it is.*

CHAPTER 7
GUILT—IT'S ALL MY FAULT

*Put down your baggage of guilt. It
was never yours to carry.*

-Unknown

Close on the heels of blame and fear rides the
nasty emotion of guilt, aka self-blame. There
are so many things to feel guilty about when
your child is a heroin addict. Almost immediately
from the moment you realize you have an addict in
the family, the guilt begins to creep in.

For whatever reason, a mother will take the blame
and suffer the guilt that goes along with it. *My son is
a heroin addict—I did something wrong. Or did I not
do enough? Did I give him too much? Too little?* All of
these questions and more scroll through your mind
like credits at the end of a bad movie.

There were many days when Dylan walked in the house and that overwhelming guilt would hit me like a ton of bricks. Even though somewhere in the rational part of my mind I knew his addiction was not my fault, my heart was broken for my son and, as his mother, I had to accept part of the blame. Every chance I got, I hugged him and reminded him how much I love him while silently asking for forgiveness. I prayed that whatever I had done wrong to cause his drug addiction would be forgiven and a solution would be put in my hands. I was wracked with guilt for a very long time.

Does any of this sound familiar? *If only I had done things differently when he was growing up. I should have paid more attention to him, given him more, talked to him more. Something traumatic must have gone wrong in his childhood that I was totally unaware of. What kind of mother am I to have missed something so important in my child's life?* It goes on and on.

There are no answers to these tortuous wonderings and questions.

This is how the heavy burden of a mother's guilt grows and grows.

That's what a mother does. We take on all the emotions, including guilt, when our child is an addict. To see him in pain and hurting from this wretched disease and to know we didn't protect him from it is probably one of the greatest types of guilt a mother will ever experience.

When we're engulfed by these emotions, we forget that we're human. We tend to push aside our very human needs and foibles. We believe, on some level, that we are superhuman, able to fix everything, save everyone, and above all else, save our children from all evils, at all costs. That's our job, isn't it?

We know we are human—obviously. But we don't really acknowledge it. Probably one of the most difficult times in our lives is when we realize that we have no special powers, we cannot control the universe, and most of all, we cannot protect our children from life's curve balls. No matter how hard we try or how carefully we manipulate their environment or control what's happening around them, it's a sobering moment when we, as mothers, realize, we aren't omnipotent. But I'm a mother! I'll kick ass and ask for forgiveness later when it comes to my children. That's my obligation as a mother...isn't it?

No.

When they're very little, we do our best to protect them, teach them, guide them, and, most of all, love them. But children grow. Children develop minds of their own. Children are influenced by experiences, people, the outside world. They're individuals, and that's exactly what we raised them to be, isn't it? They will think for themselves, they'll make decisions on their own, and sometimes, like it or not, they may not be the best or smartest decisions. But they are their own. Their decisions are not ours to make.

GUILT SERVES NO ONE

Possibly at the top of a mother's list of Hardest Things to Do is to sit by and watch her child make his own decisions. The good ones, the bad ones, the life changing ones, and the *What the hell are you thinking?* ones. Whatever the outcome, the consequences or the rewards, we have to let them own their decisions. We raised our children the best we knew how with the tools we had. We can't take on the guilt or the glory for the decisions they eventually make. They are their own people. We taught them right from wrong, we prayed for them, we educated them. But in the end, it's **their journey**, not ours. When we finally come to this truth and let go, so too will we let go of the guilt.

Fly or fall, they have to reap the rewards or suffer the consequences of decisions *made by them*. We don't have special powers or magical cures to prevent bad decisions. Let them walk their journey. We didn't *cause* their addiction, and we can't *cure* it.

I encourage you to look at the guilt you're carrying as a mother. Who told you everything would be your fault once you became a mom? It's not true, it certainly isn't fair to you, and it definitely is not helping anyone, especially you. See the guilt for what it truly is: unrealistic expectations and impractical beliefs we placed on ourselves when we gave birth. This only set us up to believe that, if something goes wrong, it must be our fault.

You are a loving, compassionate, empathetic human being who was fortunate enough to give birth to another human being who has thoughts, ideas, and choices all his own. Don't hold on to guilt. Don't blame yourself.

Of all the research on addiction out there, I have never seen any literature that states *addiction is a direct cause of a mother's love.* It's not our fault. Our children are human and, unfortunately, sometimes the disease of addiction is part of being human.

Take a deep breath and let go of the guilt.

ADDICT'S GUILT

I admit I never even gave it much thought that an addict would also suffer guilt. Through the years I learned the role guilt plays in addiction as I watched the wave Dylan rode many times. In his clear-headed moments, he was crippled with guilt because of his drug use to the point where he couldn't handle the remorse. The guilt was just another catalyst to self-medicate, and so the viscous cycle repeated itself.

Drug addicts are human too. They are very aware of feeling guilt over the trauma they have inflicted on themselves and the ones they love. They blame themselves and probably see themselves as failures. They aren't proud to be drug addicts. It's not what they ever aspired to be. They had dreams and goals that one day got totally side-railed because of their choices. They know what they have done and who they have hurt. They know the difference between *right* and *wrong*. The guilt of their decisions and negative actions eats away at them until they use drugs so they don't have to *feel* or until they are ready to face those emotions in recovery.

Guilt and shame are a huge part of addiction and play an even larger role in recovery. I mention it here so moms can try to understand that they are not alone in feeling guilt. The next time you are taking on the guilt for your addicted child, stop and remember the tremendous weight of guilt he is also carrying. This baggage isn't helping anyone, not mom nor the addict. But at least one of you can begin to pave the path to letting it go.

*Please give me the courage to let go of the guilt
I have taken on about my son's addiction.
Remind me daily that it is not my fault.
Continue to give me the strength
and knowledge to know
that I am a good mother.
Help me today to work through my feelings of guilt
and to choose happiness instead.
I ask this for my highest and greatest good.
And so it is.*

CHAPTER 8
ANGER—NOW I'M REALLY PISSED

*Without rain, nothing grows. Learn to
embrace the storms in your life.*

—Unknown

Anger has many contexts. We can be angry at
ourselves, other people, things we hear, we can
even be angry at the world. We can be angry
because things go wrong, because bad things happen
to good people, at our inabilities, our insecurities,
our shortcomings, the list goes on and on. Believe
me, you'll feel angry at everyone and everything when
your child is a drug addict. Each day brings with it
new reasons to be angry and new targets for your rage.

WHO ARE YOU MAD AT?

First and foremost, as mothers, we naturally feel anger towards our child for being a heroin addict. Even though we want to be supportive and loving, somewhere deep inside us, we are pissed off at our child for using drugs. *How dare he do this to himself? To the family! To me!*

He's destroying his life, tearing us apart, how could he? How could we not be mad?

Then we're mad at ourselves. *Where did I go wrong? What did I do? What didn't I do? How could I be so stupid? I'm a failure.* And on and on. We walk around with a chip on our shoulder, mad at ourselves, and taking it out on everyone else.

And then there's the family. *Why aren't they making him stop? Why aren't they talking to him about his problem? Why am I the only one trying to do something about it?*

More times then I care to remember, I begged his father to "do something." I wanted him to fix it. I wanted him to make it all go away. At the very least, I wanted him to talk some sense into Dylan. But no matter how much I pleaded, screamed, or cried, he seemed to just do nothing. In my opinion, he wasn't doing enough to help his son. He was too mad to talk to him, too scared to worry about it, and too stressed to sit down and have a conversation with me about it. I slowly watched the rift between us become a giant crevasse.

When he finally got tired of hearing me vent about our son, his response shot through me: "Who says you're right and I'm wrong?" That's probably when I realized we were seeing Dylan's addiction from two different perspectives, and it was no use trying to "team up" on this one. There was so much anger that we couldn't see our way through it.

What Dylan's father couldn't understand was, I never felt I was *right*. I just knew I was doing *something*, while he was doing *nothing*. That was unacceptable. And it pissed me off.

The reasons to be angry at your family members are endless. The folks closest to you are an easy target. Don't we always turn our emotions loose on those we love the most? It's natural. Fortunately for us, our family loves us back and is there for us and forgives us for the outbursts. They see the good, the bad, and the ugly. And as I can attest, during this time, there could be much **ugly** coming out of us. Try to remember, it's no one's fault. No one is to blame. But it makes us feel better to get mad and vent. Just try to do it with compassion for others' feelings.

Then there are the extended family members, community members, friends, and acquaintances who just say the stupidest things. Seriously, who would ever walk up to a mother and say, "Why aren't you doing something to help him?" I hope I would never say something so ignorant. I'd like to think I would not be that judgmental, that naïve, or that rude to a parent of an addicted child. A struggling parent who was in pain.

As the old saying goes, "Don't judge me until you've walked in my shoes" and man, isn't that the truth? As I've already noted several times, those folks who aren't in your shoes as a mother of an addicted child have no clue what you deal with on a daily basis nor do they understand the pain, confusion, and heartbreak you're feeling. They aren't trying to be cruel by saying dumb things or asking ridiculous questions about your child, the heroin addict. They just don't understand, and by the grace of God, they haven't been in your shoes.

Naturally, we feel offended and angry towards those who judge us or don't understand what our child is going through. Well, once again, I'm here to remind you, you have no time or precious energy to spend on these people. Your child is in the throes of addiction. It's not about *those people*. It's not about trying to explain, justify, or defend. Don't waste your efforts. Not now. It's truly not important. Because in all likelihood, these same people who are judging or commenting are probably scared. They are scared to death that it could be their child next. If it could happen to you, it could happen to anyone. Heroin doesn't discriminate. Their ignorant comments and questions are their way of asking, "What do I do before it affects my child, too?"

WHAT ANGER CAN DO FOR YOU

Anger serves a purpose though. It can be a great motivator. It fuels our strength and our drive to **do something.** We might not know exactly what to do or how to do it in order to help a child with an addiction, but the anger keeps us pushing. It propels us forward to just get through the day. It doesn't allow us the luxury to just give up and become immobile. It motivates us to a) acknowledge there is a problem and that's why we're angry and b) get through one more day without losing our minds. And every day you can push through is one more day closer to seeing your child begin their recovery.

Anger directed at other people—remember what we said about blame in chapter 6—is not helpful. Even unleashed rage that is directed at the universe or the problem at hand can cause damage to those around us. When we erupt in rage, we create emotional shrapnel that everyone feels. Using anger as fuel is okay, but see it for what it is.

Anger is not pretty but it's real, and it's normal. When you feel pissed off at the situation, go for a walk and scream at the clouds, do push-ups, hit your pillow, write it down… get it off your chest. And then turn around and use that same anger to move you, motivate you, and carry you forward.

I caution you here, Mom. As angry as you may feel, remember to keep communicating. Not only with those closest to you who can willingly support you in your time of need, but also with your addicted child.

Too often I became so angry with Dylan that I shut down. At times, I became so incredibly angry that I ignored him and his behaviors. This doesn't help anyone. Don't let the anger cut off conversation. You're mad, but you still love your child, and he needs you to keep talking to him. Let him know you're mad and struggling to work through it, but keep those channels open. Don't shut him out. You may be the only strength he has right now.

USE IT AND LOSE IT

Unfortunately, anger is only one of the many emotions that will arrive on your doorstep when your child becomes a drug addict. Ride through this wave the best you can but use that emotion for good. Sounds contradictory, I know. Use anger for good? Yes, that's exactly what I mean. Don't let it get the best of you, don't let it deter you, don't let it hurt the people you love, and don't let it stop you from loving and supporting your child. Use the anger as it is intended, and then let it go or it will devour you and your loved ones. Trust me, there are many more emotions to come, don't exhaust yourself with this one.

*I ask you for the strength to help me
work through my anger today
and to understand it's normal to feel angry
when addiction strikes the family.
Thank you for helping me to release my anger
and replace it with forgiveness.
Please guide me as I continue to let go of anger
and move closer to peace.
I ask this for my highest and greatest good.
And so it is.*

CHAPTER 9
GRIEF – WILL I SURVIVE THIS PAIN?

*Not until we are lost do we begin
to understand ourselves.*

—*Henry David Thoreau*

It was such an easy pregnancy. An ordinary labor and birth. At nine pounds, ten ounces, 22 inches long, Dylan was considered a "big" baby. A big, beautiful, chubby, happy, loud baby. He was so good-natured—which was a blessing since Sierra, his two-year-old sister, liked to pretend he was her real live doll. He liked his bottle and his "paci" even more. He had the most adorable dimples and a deep down from-the-gut giggle, and, by his first birthday, he sported the most gorgeous head of white blonde hair. (To this day he still has beautiful blonde hair most women envy.) Being only two years apart, he and his sister were best of friends.

As he grew up, he was quiet, but friendly. His laid-back personality won him friends and attention. He was smart and likeable. In the third grade he was honored with the prestigious award of Student of the Year at his private Catholic school. Basketball, soccer, tee-ball, baseball, football, he played them all throughout the years, always giving his all. He even ran some 5K races later on. BMX bikes, minibikes, go-karts, and eventually motorcycles (loud, fast motorcycles) became his favorite pastime.

Oldest son, younger brother, older brother, grandson, nephew, best friend, boyfriend, college student, drummer, handsome guy, landscaper, hard worker, music lover, dog lover, introvert, comedian, sweetheart—some of the many roles that defined Dylan. The one label he never appeared quite comfortable with yet owned freely was drug addict. Or "junkie" as he referred to himself later on in the years. I cried the first time I heard Dylan call himself a junkie and, I still cringe at that term. It invokes disgusting, degrading images in my head. But, let's be real, there's nothing pretty about heroin addiction. My son never pretended to sugarcoat it.

A Natural Response

Grief is a response to the loss of someone or something close to us. I guess the anger I described earlier is there to protect us from the profound grief that comes in its wake. As mothers of drug addicts, we grieve our loss.

Addiction is lonely (for the addict and for the family), but I forced myself to put a smile on my face, and one foot in front of the other and keep pushing forward. I think I finally understood why Dylan's favorite saying always appealed to me: **"Keep on keepin' on."**

Meanwhile, I mourned the son I lost. The beautiful, happy, funny, sweet son I raised. I lost him to a stranger who lies, and steals, and hides from the world. There was a grieving process I definitely went through. It caused depression and made me cry and feel hopeless. It made me hide from the world. I didn't want to go out. I didn't want to see people. I didn't want to talk to anyone. I just wanted to stay in the solace of my home and hide. I needed the comfort of the "known." As bad as things were at home, I felt most at ease (if I can even call it that) when I was in my house hiding from the outside world. At least there, in my familiar surroundings, I knew what to expect—somewhat. I had already closed myself off from family and friends. I just didn't have the energy or patience to explain addiction. People didn't get it.

Many didn't seem to *want* to get it. And I didn't have the strength (yet) to elucidate that my son was slowly dying from this wretched disease, and so was Mom.

I had to give myself time to grieve the loss of my son to heroin. No, he wasn't dead, but he might as well have been. The son I raised and knew was gone. In his place was a stranger. A shell of a boy who came and went like a ghost, rarely interacting with his family, never talking about everyday things, smiling, laughing, or enjoying life. I had to grieve what I had lost. And it hurt like hell.

IT'S NEVER GOING TO BE THE SAME

I knew I would never again see the son I once knew. He was gone, and I had to accept the loss. Even if he recovered from his addiction, he would never be the same Dylan. Addiction changes a person and too much had been lost to expect that the same son I once knew would rise up again out of this experience. That was just too much to hope for. It was another unrealistic expectation that I recognized and grieved. Of course, he still had his core values (I hoped) and his beautiful qualities that made him special inside of him, but he would never be that innocent young boy I once knew. How could he be when he had seen the depths of hell? Addiction had changed him forever, and neither of us would ever be the same.

I couldn't sleep, I had no energy to do much of anything, I cried often. I felt lonely, and empty, and overwhelmingly sad. His father and I were non-communicative. We didn't see eye to eye on addiction. I don't know if he ever fully understood or accepted how serious Dylan's addiction was. The difference between a mom and a dad? Maybe. But the lack of *togetherness* was taking its toll, and I had made the decision to fight this with Dylan on my own. If his dad couldn't be part of the solution, I'd find the answer in my own way. It left me feeling alone and isolated.

I wanted to hide inside myself when I did go out in public. God forbid I should run into someone I knew, and they wanted to stop and chat. I no longer had the energy to pretend I was happy or to make small talk. I had no strength to act like everything was okay. I felt as if I was dying on the inside while I watched my son die on the outside. There were days it was overwhelming, there were days it was scary, and there were days it felt unbearable.

With the grief came the feeling of desperation. I didn't want to watch him fight his demons anymore. I didn't want to feel his pain another day. I didn't want to feel the stress, the tension, the worry, the hurt. I literally just wanted to stay in my house and GIVE UP. Surrender to this miserable life that heroin had created. Cave under the sadness in the family, the tension in the house, and the fear of the unknown.

I felt helpless and powerless. Well, I was powerless, who am I kidding? It was a very low and dark time. Broken hearts truly do feel pain, and I was living proof.

RISE UP

Somehow, one day, the mom in me rose up. I don't know where the strength came from, but eventually I stopped feeling sorry for myself and for my son the heroin addict, and I fought my way through the grief. My heart still hurt, but I picked myself up, lifted my chin, and I faced the world. I was done hiding, done grieving, and done feeling pitied. It wasn't helping anyone.

That phase of grief was something I had to go through, and I had to give myself time for it. No, I'm certain it can't compare to burying a child, but it's still a profound loss. I had seen the son I knew and loved fade away, and I had to accept that. And it was worthy of my grief.

Then I did what I do best. I stood tall, with my head held high, and I marched out into the world to start searching for help. I had to learn everything I could about heroin. It was time to stop being held captive to this damn drug, stop being a victim, and start fighting back. The attitude I went forward with was, *Screw you, heroin, you're no match for this mother.*

It was time to get tough, it was time to fight, and it was time to get my son back.

Your grief shouldn't alarm you. It's a normal process. There are various stages of grief, and guess what some of those stages are called? Denial (the first stage of grief), anger, and depression. All of these emotions are part of the process of grief when we experience loss. They are also some of the intense emotions we go through when addiction hits home. I believe that feeling such grief during these times only confirms the notion that we have such a great capacity to love our children.

GRIEF ▶ ACCEPTANCE

Grieving can be very cleansing once you allow yourself to move through it. In hindsight, I realize I had to grieve before I could truly accept what was happening to my child.

NO, you're not crazy. You're not selfish. You're a mother. You have every right to grieve. But try not to lose yourself in the meantime. Take the time to work through the grief. Grieve because your addicted child will never be the same. But don't give up. Instead, get up! Get moving, talk to people, seek out other moms who have been where you are and know what you're going through. Do whatever you have to do to get out of the blue haze you're living in. Just make a commitment to start living again. You'll be stronger than ever.

Once you make the decision to live your life, everything starts to change. Isn't this what you're hoping your child will eventually choose?

*Please guide me through my pain and help me to see
that it's normal to feel this intense grief.
Please give me the strength to let it go and heal.
Help me to remember that my son's drug addiction
cannot control my life.
I am grateful every day for the
power to move forward.
I ask this for my highest and greatest good.
And so it is.*

CHAPTER 10
FAMILY—IT'S EVERYTHING

*Even when a mother's soul is tired, she
finds strength for her family.*

-Unknown

O h, the countless books and articles that have
been written about the effects of addiction
on the family covering such concepts as:
it's a family disease, it impacts the entire family, the
silent rules of an addicted family, etc. The literature
goes on and on. It's all in black and white, it's all
important, and it's all worth exploring. But until
heroin touches your family, there is really nothing in
print that can accurately describe the hell your family
will go through. There are no words to capture the
anguish, the heartache, the fear, and the helpless-
ness each family member will experience during the
journey through addiction. Nor can the literature

clearly identify and illustrate how each individual in the family will react to the circumstances spiraling around them.

One thing cannot be stressed enough—*addiction is a family disease.* Nothing could be truer. There may be only one person addicted, but the whole family suffers.

When your child is a heroin addict, various family members are affected in so many ways. They, too, experience the fear, anger, resentment, embarrassment, guilt, as well as a barrage of other emotions, but there are other experiences the family will struggle with as well.

EFFECTS ON FAMILY

There are the finances. Did your child steal from you to buy heroin? Have you been covering his bills since he's using his money on drugs? Have you spent an immeasurable amount of savings on legal fees or rehabilitation costs? There are many reasons why a family in addiction will feel the pinch financially. Unfortunately, the other children may even have to go without while the family finances are being funneled to the addict's needs.

Not only will the emotional wellbeing of individual family members be turned upside down, but possibly even their physical health. Yes, the stress of addiction in the family can very readily cause physical issues. The constant worry, the lack of sleep, and the everyday drain can take its toll on our health. Unfortunately, no one ever says, "Prepare yourself, get in shape, get fit, eat right, take care of yourself; you're going to need to be in the best shape of your life to deal with the stress coming at you from addiction in the family."

I know too well the physical consequences of stress. Because I had no appetite and barely slept, I lost an unhealthy amount of weight. I neglected my own thyroid issues. Who has time for that? The change in my skin and hair was not lost on me or those around me. I didn't look *healthy* because I wasn't healthy. The stress was consuming me emotionally and physically. Many times I looked in the mirror without recognizing the person looking back at me.

And then there's the emotional strain on the relationships in the family. It goes without saying, your relationship with your addicted child will run the gamut of emotions and highs and lows depending on the particular day. But other relationships within the family will suffer as well. Tensions are high, everyone's on edge, normal every day routines are constantly interrupted due to the addict's "needs". Everyone is a little short on patience at this point. There's probably an overall mood in the house of just plain negativity. The addict is the prevailing topic, even if unspoken, it's on everyone's mind and in everyone's fears.

I became very adept at reading my children's facial expressions. They didn't have to say a word or even try to articulate what they were feeling. If Dylan was having a particularly rough day, I could see by the look on Trey's face that he was just pissed off with the whole situation by now. On days that I was totally out of sorts because I realized I had money stolen from me again, one look at Jensen would convey his feelings of frustration and impatience with his brother. And on the worst of days when the sadness overwhelmed me, the mood permeated everyone in the house. Addiction was driving our emotions, our thoughts, and our fears.

Sadly, as Dylan's addiction propelled forward, extended family and acquaintances eventually stopped asking about him. They didn't ask how he was, where he was, or what he was up to. It was like he just didn't exist anymore. I never really knew if it was out of respect for me that they didn't want to bring it up, thinking they were doing me a favor, or if it was to protect themselves from the discomfort of the situation.

Family gatherings, holidays, weddings, college graduations all came and went while everyone ignored the elephant in the room. Everyone skillfully avoided talking about the addict and pretended everything was normal. Just another happy family event or memory being made. Regardless of their rationalization, people forgot about him. If they had only realized what a little empathy and compassion would have meant to our family. But, as I've noted, addiction is a lonely disease.

YOUR SPOUSE/PARTNER

You'll probably argue with your spouse over what to do and how to help your addicted child. No one knows exactly what to do or what will happen next so everyone is on edge. We often take the anxiety borne of uncertainty out on those closest to us. Maybe you'll grow apart from your partner because you're so busy putting the addict first. Your life revolves around his behaviors, his issues, and basically, keeping him alive. Meanwhile, your other relationships will suffer.

SIBLINGS

If there are younger siblings in the home, they will feel a multitude of emotions. They may feel anger towards the addict. They may feel jealousy because their sibling is getting all the attention. They may feel ignored or as if their needs are just not important to the family. Sometimes the siblings, or one of them, will begin to act out in order to regain some of the missing attention. They might get in trouble in school or start doing things they have never done before such as wet the bed, throw tantrums, withdraw, or lose themselves in video games or TV. They will feel scared because they don't understand what is really going on.

It became very clear to me what was happening with our other children. Whether it was a conscious decision or not, they stayed out of my way *and* Dylan's way. They kept quiet and asked no questions. They stayed out of sight when they felt the mood in the house warranted it.

It was a couple of years later that Trey, our youngest son, admitted to me, "I tried not to cause you more stress. I just wanted to do the right thing." I was so proud of him for having this awareness and maturity, but also sad that he felt the need to protect his parents from more hurt.

In hindsight, I realize that I suspected all along that this was what Trey was doing. By earning good grades, excelling on the track team, serving as president of his class, he was trying to be the light in a very dark time for his family. And he succeeded.

Although I know this experience with his addicted brother has changed his life in ways I may never fully understand, Trey has continued to be the warmhearted, loving beacon of positivity he aspired to be.

Jensen, our middle son, also stepped up to lighten the atmosphere. A natural-born comedian and extremely articulate, he made us laugh when we thought we could barely smile. He discussed and debated about various topics with us, leaving us feeling like he had taught us more than the other way around. He knew that he could help us, if only for fleeting moments, to forget the negativity surrounding our family. To this day, whenever I visit Jensen, I leave feeling lighter and my heart fuller.

Our youngest daughter, Sage, was too young to understand addiction in the beginning. But as time went on, she learned bits and pieces of what her oldest brother was going through. Unfortunately, she kept herself from asking questions for fear of stirring the pot. I did my best to reassure her that everything would be okay again very soon. But her heart was sad and she missed Dylan terribly the months he was away at rehab. She was always sure to mention him in her bedtime prayers, asking for him to "get healthy and come back home." She still continues to have a special bond with her big brother.

Sierra, our first-born, also did her part not to cause us more stress. While she was away at college, she was vigilant about checking on Dylan. She was always concerned with how I was holding up as well. In her quiet way, she became a pillar of strength. She would point out the obvious – both good and bad – when I was too blind with emotion to see it. I have no doubt that what she witnessed her dear brother go through helped shape her into the kind, warm, independent, non-judgmental woman she is today. But I know, deep inside, her heart still hurts for Dylan.

Siblings witness emotional outbursts from their parents which in itself is upsetting and scary. But most importantly, and sadly, they often just try to stay out of the way while everyone deals with the addict. They try to piece together what they hear and what they see and come to their own conclusions. The fear of the "unknown" is what weighs most heavily on them. And, they feel conflicted. After all, it's their sibling. Someone they love and truly want to support. On the other hand, they recognize what he's doing to the family, and they wrestle with the anger and resentment they're feeling.

Of course, as good moms, we try to mediate. We feel that we are the glue holding our tattered family together. We want to protect the addict from his siblings' opinions, fears, and anger, while at the same time we want to shelter the other children from the storm of addiction. But the truth is, one way or another, addiction is going to affect every member of the family.

Natural development seems to be curtailed in some ways by having an addicted sibling. Whether your other children act out or try to help by flying under the radar, their life-path is altered. It becomes part of their journey.

DECIDING WHAT TO DO IN A HOME WITH CHILDREN

Though addiction is a *family disease*, our actions matter immensely. How we choose to handle addiction in the family can make a huge difference in the impact on family members. And, you guessed it…most likely it will be the moms who "handle" it.

I remember quite vividly the phone call I received just prior to Dylan's committing to recovery and entering rehab the second time. Dr. Lennon had been working with Dylan for a few years. He required substance abuse counseling and prescribed Suboxone which provides relief from heroin cravings in patients trying to stay clean. Dr. Lennon recognized that Dylan was spiraling out of control with his drug use and had called that day to strongly recommend that I have Dylan leave our home. His words were, "He's going to die, and you don't want your younger children to find him dead in your house. Protect yourself and your family." Those words hit me like a freight train. Emotion pulsed through me: shock, fear, confusion, even anger—how dare he say such a thing?

I followed up that conversation with a phone call to Anna, Dylan's counselor. I was desperate to hear her say the doctor was wrong. I was praying she would tell me the situation was not as dire as Dr. Lennon made it seem. Unfortunately, Anna confirmed his warning. She explained that my son's drug use had progressed to the point where they felt his reckless behavior would soon end in his demise. She also highly suggested we tell him to leave the house. She delivered the same message as the doctor: "It's time for you to protect yourself." The words still ring horribly in my ears.

It seemed Dylan had hit his "rock bottom." How I learned to despise those words. *Rock bottom.* But here I was faced with the ugly truth—my own son's rock bottom might possibly be a coffin. Though I had lived in fear of this possible end all along, the truth of it was still a violent shock. And now I had an important decision to make: let him remain in his home where he might overdose and risk trauma to his siblings, or, kick him out and allow him to risk death on his drug dealer's floor.

No mother, anywhere, at any time, should be confronted with this crucial decision. It tortured me to face these choices. Hardest of all was the realization that, unless something changed, my son, a heroin addict, was probably going to die. Facing that reality shook me to my soul.

I considered my "options" while struggling to make the right decision. I told his father what I was wrestling with but he didn't seem to have an opinion on it. Through much prayer and meditation, I finally went to Dylan. I explained what his doctor and counselor had told me and that I was struggling with what needed to be done. Telling him that these professionals whom he respected feared his death was one of the hardest things I've ever had to do. I explained that my family needed protection. My whole family.

THE HARDEST THING IN THE WORLD

So, full of unconditional love and strength that I didn't realize I possessed, I explained my decision to Dylan. I loved him with all of my heart, but if he was going to continue to use drugs, I could no longer allow him to come back to our home. He would have to find his own place to use drugs as I would not tolerate that behavior any longer.

My head told me what his decision would be, but my heart kept unfailing hope that this just might be the wake-up call he needed. Perhaps this rock bottom, losing his beloved childhood home would be a blessing in disguise. *His* blessing. I've heard how rock bottom can be fertile ground for change for some. I prayed it would be for Dylan, too.

As hard as it was, I was doing this not just for my son, but for the family I had to protect from his behaviors. So why didn't I do this sooner, you're thinking? Good question. In hindsight, I realize I could have taken the tough love route long before Dylan's doctor enlightened me. But I wasn't ready. I hadn't hit **my** rock bottom yet. I was unable to face the possibility of having my own son dying in the street like an unwanted, thrown away piece of garbage.

But when I was ready, I acted. Our processes are as complex as those of our addicted children. Hindsight is easy but be patient with yourself. Your path will unfold as mine did but in its own way, in its own time. We just pray we are ready for the next step when we need to be.

Although it was one of the toughest moments in my own journey, I told him he had to leave.

WHERE'S THE REAL ROCK BOTTOM?

He left. And guess what? I almost lost him. Twice. Exactly as I'd feared, he overdosed.

The first time it was on his drug dealer's floor. The next time, he was in a car with the doors locked.

It was about dinner time. The phone rang. Before I even lifted the phone, I felt the hairs on the back of my neck stand straight up. *Oh God*, I thought. Somehow, I knew.

"Hello?" said a breathless voice. It was Dylan's girlfriend's mother. I'd never met her and she had no reason to call me, unless…

My heart began that familiar pounding I had come to loathe. I cut her off: "What's wrong?"

"Dylan is out in my driveway locked in his car. The windows are rolled up and we can't get it open. We can't wake him."

As I screamed to his father to get the car, I could barely compose myself.

"Is he breathing?"

"His head is slumped over. I've banged on the door and window and shouted his name. He won't move."

It should have occurred to me to call 911! But the mom in me took over. I needed to get to my son. I had to save him! That was my only thought.

The five-minute drive to their house seemed to take days. He was coming to just as we arrived, though clearly very high and still out of it. I don't think he even knew where he was or what all the commotion was about, but he was lucid enough to vehemently refuse to go to the emergency room. In his oblivion, he failed to comprehend the direness of the situation—or how close he came to not waking up. But there is no arguing with an addict when his mind is made up.

I pleaded with his father, "We have to take him. Don't listen to Dylan." Unfortunately, he chose to oblige his son. He didn't argue the fact that he might need medical attention, he simply kept quiet and drove home.

Are you freaking kidding me? Was what screamed in my brain. But it was two against one, and it became apparent that I wasn't winning this argument. So, we went home where Dylan could sleep off his drug-induced fog, while I coped with my fury, and his father could retreat to his silence. Dysfunction at its best. *Why was I the only one who could see this?*

By the grace of God, Dylan's life was spared. The power of my prayers was evident to me. These overdoses scared him enough that he finally sought help. I still thank God every day for allowing him to survive those near-death experiences. My decision to make him leave the house precipitated his true rock bottom and the beginning of his road to recovery. Thankfully, my family, especially his younger siblings, were spared the frightening experience of finding their brother overdosed in their home.

So why am I telling you all this? Because I know that some of you have been faced with decisions like this one. It's an unfair, gut-wrenching place to be as a mom. It feels as if you're being asked to make a choice between your addicted child and the rest of the family. No mom wants to make that choice. But it's so important to remember to protect yourself and your family when there is an addict in your midst. You love your addicted child deeply, but you can no longer allow him to hurt everyone else. The addict isn't the only one caught in a trap. The time comes when you do what you think is best to save your whole family.

The effects of addiction on family members, especially siblings, can be deep and lasting.

It's more than discomfort and unhappiness. When children need to cope with an addicted sibling, their behaviors may totally change in an attempt to adjust to what's happening. And then those behaviors can possibly interfere with healthy functioning later in life.

As moms, we want to set all our children up for success, and sometimes we must make brutally painful decisions about an addicted child in order to do what's right for our other children. Plus, remember enabling? By giving Dylan a home, despite the hurtful behaviors that arose from his addiction, I was enabling him. And that had to stop.

My decision to kick Dylan out of the house was not about loyalty or who I loved more. It was about drawing the line, setting limits, and detaching myself and my family "with love" from the chaos of an addict still bent on self-destruction.

HOLDING SPACE FOR THE FAMILY

We moms have a responsibility to our families to **be honest and to be present.** That means we need to talk to the children in our home and explain what's going on with the addicted sibling. Once children know and understand (as much as they can understand depending on their age), they'll feel some relief and probably appreciate the honesty. They have a right to know what's happening, and we do them a disservice by keeping such important secrets.

Sit them down, talk to them, explain what's going on, answer their questions, but most of all listen to their concerns, their questions, their fears, and whatever else they want to talk about. Be present. Hold space. They deserve our undivided attention, too.

Once Dylan was in rehab and working on his recovery, I called a family meeting with his brothers, his sisters, father, and other family members. These are the people I felt were closest to Dylan as he was growing up. While my well-intentioned reason for this meeting was to explain to the family how my son needed their love and support now more than ever, it turned out I got a lot more than I bargained for. I learned much more about my family and how Dylan's addiction had impacted the impressionable lives of his sisters and brothers. It was eye-opening, informative, and upsetting, but at the same time, it was uplifting and cleansing. Now that he was getting the help he needed, everyone was more open about how it affected them. They were released by their relief, and shared openly, and spoke their minds, asked questions, and unburdened themselves of feelings and worries they had been keeping inside for far too long.

So, what exactly did I learn?

Sierra had been pissed off for quite some time at her brother whom she adored, and with whom she was very close growing up. She was mad because he didn't reach out to her to talk about his addiction. "He just drifted away once he started using drugs. He didn't reach out to me. He didn't want to talk to me about it." She took this personally and didn't really understand it. And she was a little mad at me, too. On some level she thought her mom could fix it all and make it go away. Since I couldn't do that, she felt scared and angry at me for a perceived failure, even while she was old enough to know that wasn't logical. Our fear-based emotions never are.

Trey was very confused about addiction and asked some great questions. "I don't understand how addiction works. Look at all the time, energy and money you and Dad have spent on his addiction. And he keeps doing it." Again, the underlying emotion with him seemed to be resentment. But he was also uncertain about the role he should play in his brother's recovery process.

Jensen expressed quite eloquently how his oldest brother's addiction had left its mark on him: "I would have loved to have my older brother growing up. I didn't because he was lost in his world of drugs." He was right. It just hadn't occurred to me that he (all of my children) had grown up without their brother. Sure, he was physically with them, but he wasn't really present once his experiences with drugs began. His siblings didn't have many opportunities to interact with or get to know their brother on a meaningful level.

They were all hurting. How the hell did I miss that? Easy. I was too absorbed in the disorder addiction had brought to our lives. The confusion and the fear consumed me so thoroughly that I wasn't capable of recognizing how my children were feeling.

I was so grateful that day to hear them, learn from them, and open myself to their questions, concerns, and emotions. As their mom, I needed to hear them. I needed to understand that their young lives were still progressing and being influenced, and their needs were just as significant as their brother's. It was one of those life-altering moments I will always remember.

SELF-CARE

It's not only your family for whom you need to be present. An important lesson here is that you must take time out for YOU. Take time to relax. Do something that you enjoy doing.

The world can't stop because your child is a heroin addict. Life must go on.

We have to push through, and we have to continue to take care of ourselves. I once worked for a boss whose mantra was, "When things get rough, put your own oxygen mask on first." Isn't that the truth! We all need to take care of **us** if we want to be available and any use at all to our family. It's important to remember that.

For me, it felt as if I had been holding my breath for far too long. For years I hadn't relaxed or let my guard down. I didn't feel that I had the right to do that. My son, a heroin addict, was suffering and he needed me. I had to be brave and vigilant and there was no time to breathe. I had to keep pushing.

As moms, we all tend to put our needs behind everyone else's. We often miss the very fact that we *have* needs! But please heed the warning. It's so important for you to care for yourself first this time. Now is the time to be a little **selfish** if that's what we have to call it. Now is the time to take care of you. Don't let the addiction in the family drag you under. Do this for your health and survival. You're no good to anyone with stress-induced health issues. You want to fight for your child? Well then you need to be in shape and ready to do just that. So, take some time right now to do what you need to do and think of you for a change. You have to remember to breathe.

What does that look like for you? You've probably forgotten what it's like to put your needs first, or to even think about what you might need. I encourage you to seek out someone to talk to. There are professionals out there for you. There are counselors and family therapists who specialize in treating people affected by a loved one's addiction. No, you're not

the first person to seek an outside, unbiased professional. This is someone who understands what you
and your family are going through and can offer you
the tools to get through it. I know you might think,
"I don't need to talk about it." Trust me, I know
that feeling. As moms, we want to be the rock, the
pillar of strength. Talking to a therapist or counselor
doesn't mean you're weak. It means you're human.
And very wise.

A therapist has a lot of experience in an area where
you are just a beginner—how to navigate this new
reality. Use that expertise to help you - and thus your
whole family, including your addicted child.

We all need some guidance in our lives, at certain
times more than others. A professional just might
be someone you can talk to who will offer some new
insight on the situation. They just might say something that strikes a chord with you and guides you to
a new way of recognizing how you can help yourself.
They aren't there to judge you or belittle you. Be
willing to reach out to someone and open enough
to tell your story. Only then can true healing begin.

There are also meetings you might seek out, such
as Al-Anon or Nar-Anon. These groups are designed
to offer the families of addicts support, education,
and an understanding of addiction as a disease, as
well as the strength to cope with the chaos created
by the addict in the family. You might be thinking

the same thing I was for years… "I don't need to hear others' negative stories about their addicted child. What good will it do me to hear the agony others are going through?" Again, I'm here to tell you, keep an open mind and seek out a meeting near you. Try it.

If nothing else, you'll quickly realize, **you are not alone.** There are many moms out there going through the same pain as you. Once you grasp this, you'll find yourself becoming more open to the support of others. These are real people living the same reality as you. They have an addicted child. They aren't there to judge or berate you. They'll offer support and encouragement, and they just might say something to help you gather the strength to push forward in a healthy manner, and to help your family recover as well. Don't kid yourself. Yes, we moms believe we are invincible, but we aren't. We all need support at some point in our lives. Don't ever be too proud to recognize that. You deserve this for yourself.

I ask you to guide my words and my actions
so that I'm able to speak honestly with
my family about addiction.
Guide my intentions while I listen
to and discuss their questions
and concerns so that they will learn
and their fears will subside.
Give me the strength and wisdom to practice self-care,
and the knowledge to understand that I
don't have to go through this alone.
Help me to remember that taking charge
of my own life is all I can do
in order to walk this journey with peace and grace.
I ask this for my highest and greatest good.
And so it is.

CHAPTER 11
EDUCATION—GET SMART

I can show you where to dig and what to dig for, but the digging you must do for yourself.

—Matisyahu

Truth be told, I should have known sooner about the perils of addiction. Why didn't I educate myself on the signs, the symptoms, the what-to-dos and what-not-to-dos? I wish I had taken the time. But who thinks they'll have to know this stuff? How many mothers decide when their children are young, "I better learn about addiction and, in particular, heroin?" Until it hits home and you find yourself in the midst of the storm, you don't give it a thought. Then you realize how little you really know about the subject and how lost you feel navigating the level six whitewater of addiction.

For example, I don't even remember when I started to keep track of "the signs." All I know is, it became an everyday activity. I watched Dylan's behaviors, his pupils, his speech, his body language. I watched for needle marks, I noticed his eye contact (or lack of), his head posture. I paid acute attention to his daily routines and activities, his eating and sleeping patterns. When he was asleep, I would watch his shallow breathing. I learned quickly enough to know when he was high. When he was awake, I could tell when he was battling the urge to use heroin again, and I knew when he was in withdrawal. I could tell how long ago he used. I noticed his increased isolation, mood swings, relentless weight loss, and even the random episodes of vomiting when he had just used.

And while all this was taking place in front of me, I was spending countless hours playing detective. I checked his cell phone for messages and calls to his drug dealers. I searched his room for paraphernalia. I tried to watch his comings and goings to figure out where the heroin was coming from. I had delusions of changing the world. I was going to get these disgusting heroin dealers and turn them in to the police. I was singlehandedly going to stop this epidemic from spiraling out of control! But first and foremost, I was going to keep Dylan alive.

What mother wants to know this stuff? Who wants to be an expert on her son's drug use? I could have lived my life not ever recognizing the signs of heroin abuse. But, it's the journey on which I had been launched without my consent.

So, I educated myself. As moms, we learn very quickly about whatever subject is thrown at us when it comes to our children. We have no choice if we hope to get through this tumultuous time in one piece. Lack of knowledge or understanding just aren't feasible excuses. We are moms. It's our responsibility to understand addiction once it hits home. Claiming ignorance while *not* reacting is not an option when you're a mom.

REALITY CHECK

I read everything I could find, every book, every article, whatever was available on the internet. I read anything out there that might give me a clue about dealing with addiction. I felt stupid, lost, uneducated, and totally ill-prepared.

I scrambled. As I began my frantic research, I looked everywhere for clues about what I was doing, what I was not doing, and/or what I should be doing. I began talking to professionals, doctors, therapists, drug counselors, other parents of addicts, anyone I thought might have some knowledge to impart on the subject of heroin addiction. It's astounding (and reassuring at the same time) how much information is available on the topic if you actually take the time to look for it.

Again, I had another reality check when I started reading and learning. So much to know, so much I did not know, and even more that I never wanted to know. But in order to support my son on a path of recovery, I had no choice. **I had to learn what I was dealing with.** In my experience, it's difficult to fight an enemy you don't know anything about. We can accomplish far more when we are armed with knowledge. That's not to say that now I know it all, but I know a lot more than I did, and it has helped me feel better equipped to deal with whatever might yet happen.

ACCEPTANCE

Being empowered with knowledge also helped lead me to…acceptance. Eventually, I stood face to face with all the facts—scientific, psychological, sociological, political, philosophical, and all the ramifications, outcomes, conclusions, complications, treatment options, cutting edge theory and research, and more. It was then that I had no choice but to accept what I was dealing with.

It wasn't enough to just be out of denial and know my son was a heroin addict. There was much more to this. The depth of it, the tragedy of it, and the reality that it may not end well. I finally had to accept the darkness that was surrounding my family and not make excuses for it. It was time for me to meet this ugly monster head on. No more hoping things would change on their own. I realized that I had to have some frank conversations with Dylan, and I accepted that I needed to be prepared for the answers. So, I set out on the next phase of this journey and began talking to the addict in front of me.

I recommend that you waste no precious time and energy on the *why*. Of course that's a burning question in the back of our minds: *why, why, why*? We may never know why our children decided to use drugs for the first time. Curiosity? Peer pressure? Rebellion? Stress? To self-medicate? Numb uncomfortable emotions? I will probably never know. I eventually did ask my son, "Why?" Unfortunately, the answer is no clearer to me.

He was kind enough to reassure me, "It wasn't anything you did Mom, you were perfect." Perfect? Far from it! But I know I tried my best with the tools I had been given, and that's all I could do. So, don't waste time trying to figure out how it all started. (Although many curious friends and family will conjecture on this. *Let them.*) Spend your energy more wisely, learning how to keep your child, the heroin addict, alive until he's ready for recovery.

WHAT IS ADDICTION?

While the theme of this book centers around the emotional aspect of living with an addicted child, I also want to share with you some of the basic information I discovered as I launched my own research into heroin addiction.

So, what is addiction anyway? Listed below are some of the important things I've picked up and come to understand. Addiction:

- ❖ is chronic
- ❖ includes characteristics such as compulsive drug-seeking behaviors and continued, uncontrolled drug use despite negative consequences
- ❖ involves strong cravings for a drug, tolerance (need to use larger amounts to get the same effect), and withdrawal symptoms
- ❖ literally changes the structure and functioning of the brain
- ❖ can be *controlled* successfully but not cured and is thus a lifelong disease
- ❖ cannot be treated with "willpower"
- ❖ is not a character defect
- ❖ does not mean a person is weak or a failure

DISEASE VS. CHOICE

Then I decided to delve further into the question: *is addiction really a disease?* Everyone, even those who are most ignorant and least armed with actual information, has an opinion about this subject. Most opinions are little more than guesses. After reading a lot of actual data-supported research, I fully support the professionals of the American Medical Association and the American Society of Addiction Medicine who define addiction as a *disease.*

That being said, I understand that it's a choice to use heroin for the first time. Maybe the second and the third time. That's undeniable. We all have free will, right? But those folks who choose to use drugs and alcohol never made the choice to *become addicts.* And, as we know, not every individual who tries drugs or alcohol becomes addicted. Many factors including our genes, our environment, socialization, trauma, and even mental illness can play a role in impelling the pendulum towards addiction.

Environment includes things such as the neighborhood we lived in, the home we grew up in, and the school we attended. It also refers to societal pressures and the stresses we face within each area of our life, and even whether some people tend to isolate more than others.

When we hear *peer pressure,* we usually think of kids growing up, and the influence of their classmates, schoolmates, and friends. But kids are not the only ones influenced by peer pressure. Though the young may find social pressure more difficult to deal with, we all have peers, no matter how old we are, at work, in our living arrangements, and in our relationships.

Therefore, we are each shaped and influenced by our peers in some fashion.

No one knows how many times a person needs to use heroin before he becomes addicted. But we do know heroin is highly addictive and continued use changes the brain. Once the brain has been altered, the drug addict has a more difficult time making good decisions and is unable to control his use or ignore the physical cravings and extreme discomfort the body experiences without the drug. Using will-power to stop using heroin is not a viable option any longer. Hence, a heroin addict is created. The disease has taken over. And for those who like to point out, "Well, he chose to use heroin," let's be very clear. There comes a point when **it is no longer a choice**, but a way of life that becomes necessary. The addict uses heroin **just to feel normal**.

I've mentioned just a few of the countless aspects of addiction to consider when you start to educate yourself. This is merely the tip of the iceberg. The more you know and understand, the stronger you will become to deal with the issues at hand.

*Please help me to learn about addiction
and what my child is suffering through.
Give me the strength to get through this day.
Guide me with pure intentions so
that I am prepared and
able to support my child in his
recovery by educating myself.
Help me to recognize that I cannot
do the work for him
and remind me that it is his journey to walk.
I ask this for my highest and greatest good.
And so it is.*

CHAPTER 12
STIGMA—BE THE CHANGE

Don't hate what you don't understand.

-John Lennon

S tigma is *a mark of disgrace associated with a particular circumstance, quality or person.* Disgrace? How sad is it that our society views a person with the disease of addiction as a "disgrace?"

Unfortunately, we're well aware of the stigma surrounding heroin addiction. Isn't it strange that we don't have stigmas surrounding people with cancer or diabetes or arthritis, but for some reason, we as a society have created this stigma around those afflicted with addiction? But, if I'm being completely honest, I was part of that culture once, too.

Before addiction struck my family, I had a preconceived notion of what a heroin addict was. If asked,

I might have used phrases and terms like, the dregs of society, jobless, homeless, bums, street people, no purpose, no use to society. They chose that life, didn't they? They could get clean and live productive lives if they wanted to, right? They must have come from really bad families.

I cringe as I write this. Remembering my uneducated opinions of drug addicts so very long ago. What makes me feel even worse is the fact that I know there are many people who still hold these opinions. But before I ridicule the non-educated, I'm quick to remind myself that they haven't been touched by addiction, thus they know no better. And for that, I'm grateful. Addiction is not something I would wish on anyone.

Ignorance is No Excuse

Remember the old adage, "Ignorance is bliss?" Well, ignorance is a luxury no one can afford. In fact, **ignorance is dangerous**. There's no good argument or excuse for society not to be aware of and educated about the facts of addiction. We all need to wake up and realize that it's a disease like many other diseases. And yes, people die from addiction. Should we hide that fact? Should we pretend it doesn't exist? Should we be afraid to tell our family and friends? Why are we so embarrassed that a DISEASE has afflicted our family? Why are we ashamed that our child is struggling with addiction?

Dylan came from a great family with two loving parents, and sisters and brothers who looked up to him. He had everything he could have wanted: a beautiful home, an education, enriching experiences, luxuries like cars, motorcycles, toys, and vacations. He had friends and girlfriends. He's smart, handsome, and extremely likeable. He's got an incredible work ethic. He was gifted with enormous love, morals, values, opportunities, invaluable experiences, and good parents.

Addiction just doesn't happen to families like ours. But guess what? My son, my firstborn male, my beautiful, loving, warm-hearted son became a heroin addict. So yes, **addiction does happen to families like ours.**

ADDICTION DOES NOT DISCRIMINATE

WHO THE HELL ARE WE KIDDING? Addiction doesn't discriminate. Addiction doesn't care what kind of family you come from, what size your house is, how much money your parents make, or whether you're a "good person" or not. Addiction happens - to anyone, anywhere, any time. Don't fool yourself into thinking it could never happen to your family. No one is exempt from the potential disaster of addiction. Why would we think we are any different? Why are we any better than anyone else? We're all human. Each one of us. And for that reason, we're vulnerable to addiction.

A few years ago, Jensen posted something on Facebook. It was the summer after he graduated from high school. It made me extremely proud. Reading it over and over, I thought to myself, "He gets it." I'm so grateful that he's an intelligent, articulate, and outspoken young man who is not afraid to speak out on important issues. Even topics that might scare most people. It's people like him who will change this world. These are his words:

"Each and every one of you reading this right now knows someone struggling with opiate addiction. If you think you don't, that's only because you're unaware of it. It's arguably the largest problem facing young people today. But for most of you, the sound of the word *heroin* makes you shudder. We live in a society that tells us not to talk about that, like it's a curse word or something. We put all our energy into avoiding the topic and hoping some magical solution will fall upon us. We do this with every scary taboo issue facing us…poverty, immigrants, racial tensions. We ignore it and through that, we marginalize the problem. Most people today don't even realize how much heroin exists in their own town, because we try so hard to ignore it and pretend like it doesn't exist. However, the magical solution we're all waiting for is already here and it's called **education**. Heroin addiction is a very real thing that is affecting every single one of our lives, and not a god damn thing is going to change until we start to talk about it."

Well said, right? He gets it. What about the rest of us? Let's stop judging those with an addiction. Let's stop judging their families. Let's stop trying to guess why someone is addicted. Let's stop judging ourselves as mothers. Accept the fact that addiction is a disease that crosses all boundaries. It doesn't differentiate based on gender, color, age, or home environment. It ignores all boundaries including those created by economic status, geography, profession, or politics.

Ask me questions. Not about my parenting skills. Ask me about my son, a heroin addict.

I'll do my best to share what I know so we can all become aware and learn about addiction. Instead of judging me or my son, how about you just support us? Don't perpetuate the stigma. Choose to be part of the solution.

BE THE CHANGE

You can help break the stigma surrounding addiction by doing what Gandhi suggested:

"Be the change you wish to see in the world."

The saying has become so cliché; however, it holds such a simple truth. We can't even effect change until we start with ourselves. Don't just *talk* about change, *be* about change. Start to break the ugly cycle of stigma. If you're hoping it's going to change, be willing to make it happen. Be the one - the one to start talking about heroin addiction. Be the one who will open others' eyes and hearts.

How many times has a mother of an addict wondered, *Why me?* Well why **not** you? Why **not** be the one to help others awaken? Why **not** be the one to step up and speak up?

Be the one who can say, "I helped change the stigma of addiction!"

I've seen firsthand how devastating the stigma is. I lived it. I felt it. And unfortunately, I helped to perpetuate it. But once I made the decision to begin to **learn,** the universe helped me change the way I viewed addiction. And then I knew I had to help stop the stigma. I had to be part of the change. I couldn't live with the walls up around the topic of addiction any longer.

I implore you to educate yourself, talk about it, talk to everyone who will listen to you, embrace it for what it is – a disease. People are dying. Our children are dying. Is keeping heroin addiction a secret helping anyone? We're so much smarter than that. The more we can educate ourselves and those around us, the faster society as a whole will begin to accept that addicts are people too. They are human beings who deserve our understanding and our support. We owe it to our children and our families to put an end to the stigma of drug addiction.

Addiction doesn't discriminate. Shouldn't society reciprocate?

COMMUNICATION

I think the stigma even causes us to struggle with open communication with our own addicted child. Addiction is so taboo and so misunderstood in general that, when confronted with it, we wrangle with how to talk about it openly. We feel conflicted, confused, ashamed. We flounder to find the words to speak with our child about their drug use. But keep in mind how important communication is.

Talk to your child. Find out what he's using, how much he's using, and where he stands in terms of wanting treatment.

I wish I had talked to my son sooner. I wish I had asked more questions. I wish I hadn't let the stigma stop me in my tracks. (I guess the *wishes* never really end.)

There were times over the years that it was so much easier for me to withdraw from the world around me rather than meet it head on. The tears flowed much more effortless than words.

For far too long, my head knew I should confront Dylan while my inconsolable heart left me speechless. The emotions were so overwhelming that they often left my good-intentioned attempts to talk to my son about his addiction in a puddle at my feet.

I do regret the precious time I wasted wallowing in my sadness instead of talking with Dylan.

Communicating can be so damn hard sometimes. Especially when it's needed the most. I know it was equally difficult for him to start the conversation. I sensed there were days he really wanted to, but he just couldn't bring himself to follow through. I could see the shame and guilt written all over his face. I knew it only made things worse for him. The vicious cycle of using drugs to medicate the self-loathing emotions his addiction brought upon himself. We were both struggling to deal with our emotions and our attempts to communicate with one another. I hope you won't waste so much time with your own addicted child.

Don't be afraid to start the conversation. His life might literally depend on it.

*Grant me the courage and the power
to walk in my own truth.
Allow me to shed light on addiction
so that others might understand
and become part of the solution.
Guide my words and my actions
so that I may be a voice to other moms
so that together we may break the stigma of addiction.
I ask this for everyone's highest and greatest good.
And so it is.*

CHAPTER 13
COMPASSION – THE WORLD NEEDS MORE

*If it's so hard for you to watch my son's addiction, imagine how hard it must be to **live** it.*

-Unknown

Compassion is sympathy and concern for the sufferings of others. Sounds simple enough. Unfortunately, this doesn't appear to be an innate human trait.

I believe that society today lacks compassion, and that lack of compassion is responsible for the stigma around addiction. We're too busy judging, talking about others, placing blame, and even fearing, *oh boy, that could be my child.* I would propose that we stop that bullshit. How about we wake up and realize **we are all in this together**.

Maybe addiction hasn't touched your child personally but don't fool yourself into thinking that it hasn't affected you. It may be a distant relative, a friend, a friend's child, a coworker's family member, your mailman, or the son of the guy riding the subway with you in the morning on the way to work who is dealing with addiction. Yes, addiction does affect us all. Have some compassion for your fellow human beings.

Stop and think for a moment: Are you perfect? None of us are. Neither are drug addicts. Do you have compassion for people who are sick? People who have a disease; those who struggle or are in pain? Well, guess what? Addicts are people, too. And they're struggling, sick, and in pain.

They're worthy of your love and compassion. So, let's quit judging them from afar. Where's the sympathy? Where's the genuine caring about other human beings? What does it say about people if all they do is kick the addict when he's down?

Don't get me wrong. I'm not saying we ought to feel sorry for drug addicts and excuse their behaviors. There's a difference. Yes, they have a disease they're battling. They deserve compassion and understanding. I won't excuse their behaviors or the things they might do to get their next fix, but I will have understanding that this is the disease taking over. Addicts will do and say things they might never imagine doing or saying if they were drug-free.

Let's just take a step off our righteous pedestals and remember, this is the addict acting out. How about we say: "It's not okay that you stole from me or lied to me over and over, but I understand that it's part of your addiction. Addiction does not define you. It doesn't make you who you are. I have compassion for the person you are, not for the things you do as an addict."

COMPASSION MUSTN'T DISCRIMINATE

Compassion is caring. That's it. In this case, it's caring about another person who happens to be afflicted with a disease. Not judging him or excusing him. Just **caring**. Understand that we're all doing the best we can with the journey we're on. Imagine what a beautiful world it would be if everyone woke up tomorrow morning with an attitude of *compassion* towards others. All others.

I came across a letter one day on Facebook from a young woman who had lost her husband to a drug overdose. Her letter was in response to someone who had posted her personal opinion about the time, energy, and cost involved in saving the lives of addicts. Clearly, that person had no patience nor compassion for those with an addiction to drugs, and did not see the need to spend resources saving those lives.

The young woman's passionate response struck me hard. I cried as I read it over and over while I applauded her gutsiness in speaking out, cheered for her loyalty to her husband, and admired her ability to genuinely articulate her feelings through her own grief. It also reflects our society's lack of compassion and understanding of the problem of addiction, most likely due to the fact that it's so rarely openly discussed.

I'm humbled and grateful to this young woman for sharing her journey. Whether she realizes it or not, she is making a difference in the world.

Dear Judgy Lady on Facebook,

I read the article you shared on Narcan. Your opinion and commentary made my pulse pound and my face flush. I was angry, but after a few minutes passed, I didn't want to punch you in the face anymore. My heart softened towards you because I know you just don't get it. You are so lucky, and I am envious of that. I wish more than anything else that I didn't get it either. I never wanted to either, and as much as I think you suck for saying what you did, I hope you never have to. You see, I know something you don't know. I have lived it, walked, and most importantly survived it while you sit on the other end of a computer content in your ignorance. I hear that it is bliss.

I made a decision early on in life not to use drugs or alcohol. It wasn't because I was a saint, it was because I was scared of it. Not having my wits about me at all times terrified me, so I abstained. I left parties early, I just said no. That old DARE pledge may have been one of the only things I have ever truly followed through with in my life. Well, the second...

I have always wanted the same thing we all want, "True Love." The heart racing, soul fucking stuff that roll-of-the-eye inducing movies are made out of. Lucky for me, I found it, and I cherished it, I protected it, I stood by it through thick and thin. It was mine and I was never letting go no matter the cost. Unlucky for me, I lost the human form of the person it was attached to. It went defunct in a rundown apartment five minutes from my house, surrounded by people who did not give a shit about that love. I lost the most precious person to me other than my children without a "goodbye" or a last "I love you." I lost the keeper of my secrets, my duet partner, my finisher of my sentences, the other half of my heart. I lost my financial stability, my security blanket, my hope, my sanity, my will to live, my plus one, and my emergency contact. I lost my home with Narcan a truck door open away.

I get it. You think it was his "choice." You think he didn't love me or anyone else enough. You think he was selfish, stupid, and weak. You think he didn't deserve your tax dollars even though he worked harder than anyone I have ever known in my life. If I told you how wrong you are, you probably will not be convinced. He is the face of a million "junkies" to you. You might not care that he poured ketchup all over his fries and ate them with a fork or that he always gave money to the homeless. That he smelled like wood chips, soap, and just the tiniest hint of a hotel swimming pool or that he could draw a blueprint with his eyes closed. You won't be moved to hear that he loved my feet, put my coat on me on our first date, and ended every text with, "I love you more than all the stars in the sky," but all of these things mattered to ME. You are basing his worth on an image you have in your head.

It just feels so important to me that you know this, there are good and bad drug addicts just like there are good and bad NON drug addicts. He would never judge you for being such an asshole. If I had gone to him all fired up and read to him what you wrote, he would chuckle and tell me to calm down. He was a better person than you and me combined.

My question to you is simply, what about me? Do I deserve your sympathy and your compassion? Is my pain any less because the person I loved was a heroin addict? Do I deserve to suffer for loving someone you don't deem worthy? Did he, for making one poor choice that led him down the road to hell? Do the obese deserve insulin or a defibrillator? Do smokers deserve chemotherapy? Where does it stop when we start making these kinds of calls?

Still I know I probably haven't changed your mind. It seems pretty set. All I can ask is that you honor my pain, just like I would honor yours if your husband dropped dead because he ate a few too many cheeseburgers. I ask that you do because we are all human and we are all in this together.

Sincerely,

The Junkie's Wife, Elizabeth Ann Grundy

Moms Need Compassion, Too

Drug addicts are not the only ones who need and deserve compassion. Mom does, too.

There are some who may always choose to judge the parents and blame them for their son's addiction. By now, I fully understand this is ignorance rearing its head. I no longer take it personally. But that doesn't mean I'll let it slide. It doesn't mean I won't take advantage of opportunities to enlighten those lacking empathy for a mom of an addict.

I was invited to dinner recently with a group of long-time friends, most of us mothers. At some point in our lovely evening, the casual conversation turned to the topic of a local girl struggling with drug addiction. I tread cautiously into those waters as I was quick to observe the undertone of disgust at the table. I guess these ladies forgot they were dining with a mom of a heroin addict because judgements and opinions were candidly being served at the table. Not only did they pass judgement on the girl addicted to heroin, but also on her "enabling mom" who was "mishandling" the entire situation.

I did my best to rebut their uneducated remarks and to help them understand addiction from the wisdom of a mom who has *been there*. Realizing soon enough that my attempts were in vain, I closed the precarious conversation by reminding them, "Until you've walked in my shoes, don't ever judge a mom's love for her child. Until you've lived my son's journey, do not dare to judge his path. You have no clue what you would do or not do, so don't speculate. Spend some time learning about addiction first, and then talk to some moms about what they are going through and what they deal with on a daily basis. Set your opinions aside and educate yourself. Open your heart instead of your mouth because the world needs so much more of that."

Moms need compassion as much as their addicted child does. We're all hurting. We're all struggling. And, we're all doing the best we can. Be the person to reach out to a mom and ask how *she* is doing. Be an ear if she needs to talk. Be a shoulder if she needs to lean on you. Compassion is caring – that is all you're asked to do.

*Please help me to feel compassion for everyone,
especially those addicted.
Help me to see another person's burden
without judgement or harsh words,
and allow me to understand that
addiction is another disease
that deserves my compassion.
Remind me daily that we are all imperfect
humans each with our own journeys.
Help me to always feel compassion
for all human beings.
I ask this for my highest and greatest good.
And so it is.*

CHAPTER 14
GRATITUDE - BRINGS PEACE

*Piglet noticed that even though he
had a very small heart, it could hold a
rather large amount of gratitude.*

—*A.A. Milne*

And finally, we get to a place of *gratitude*. It might surprise you to hear that I feel *gratitude*. You might be thinking, *Grateful? For what? My child is a heroin addict, and I should be GRATEFUL for that?* Not exactly what I mean. This chapter is for YOU, Mom. Remember what I wrote earlier about putting your own oxygen mask on before you can help your child? Well, gratitude is part of that process.

Gratitude is huge. I learned this along the way while grieving, being pissed off, and depressed. One morning I woke up, and, as was typical, didn't want to get out of bed. I didn't want to face the day. Another day of seeing my son in agony. Another day of living on knife edge of fear. *What's in store for me today?* Another day of constant prayer that my son would survive the day.

As we moms know, this isn't living. We go through the motions because we have no choice but to get up, get moving, and do what we do. We have people relying on us—families, other children, employers, employees, friends. As much as we want to stay under the covers, close our eyes, and wish the day away, we have to will ourselves to get up and go. We're moms.

GRATITUDE WASN'T ALWAYS MY ATTITUDE

I spent my days, all my hours, dwelling on the negative. I was consumed with thoughts only of Dylan's disease. Every waking moment was spent in thought or prayer about his addiction. What to do, will he survive, where is he getting the heroin, how can I convince him to get help, when will he be ready to begin recovery…the negative and fear-based thoughts went on and on, over and over, like a broken record playing in my head on a daily basis. I couldn't focus on my work, my other children, or even my own needs. My mind was stuck in a track like a stereo needle skipping and repeating on a vinyl record.

And then one day, I discovered the power of gratitude. While praying for the strength to get through one more day of the same drudgery, something hit me. It was one of those "lightbulb moments." I suddenly remembered to stop sulking in my pity for a moment and *thank* the universe for everything I had. In the midst of the extreme sadness and chaos Dylan's addiction had brought, I literally woke up and gave thanks. I had so many things to be grateful for. I had just forgotten to acknowledge them.

COUNT YOUR BLESSINGS

Dylan was alive! For that I was most grateful. I was also grateful for my other children, my health, my family and friends, our home, our jobs, the list went on and on. For all of it, I was bountifully grateful.

I thanked the universe for the strength, courage, and ability to get through each day and be there for my son as he fought his addiction. I was grateful that I was able to physically and emotionally get out of bed each morning and greet the day. I was grateful I had not completely lost my mind to worry and fear. I was truly and sincerely grateful for so many things, large and small.

From that day forward, I focused on my gratitude. Not only did I start each day giving thanks for the many blessings in my life, but in those moments throughout the day that I felt overwhelmed with fear and worry, I made a conscious effort to pause, if only for a minute. I would remember everything I had to be grateful for, and I would thank the universe right then and there for all of its goodness.

It only takes a moment to bring to mind all of the things in life we can be grateful for. For most of us, life gets so busy that we forget to make time for gratitude. But when you make just the slightest effort to recognize even the smallest things in life, you start to see how fortunate we really are.

Warm sunshine (or rain for the garden), the birds singing, trees, the food on the table, the morning coffee in your cup, the person who held the door open for you, the hugs from your family, silly jokes that make you laugh, the beauty of nature all around us, the clouds, the clothes you wear, the light that turns on when you flip that switch -- the list is endless of what we should be grateful for.

Most especially, still today every time I look at Dylan, when he doesn't know I'm watching him study or taking a nap on the couch, the feeling of gratitude overwhelms me. It fills my soul. I no longer take things for granted. I am well aware of how truly blessed I am to have my son, and I strive to embrace my blessings each and every day.

One day I started a *gratitude list* in my journal which still amazes me to this day as I continue to watch it grow as I add to it each morning.

Do you know what this new *attitude of gratitude* brought into my life? An enveloping feeling of calm and peace. Sounds corny, I know, but that's the only way I can describe it to you. My worries and fears subsided immediately as I gave thanks for my blessings in life. It was like suddenly life didn't feel quite so unbearable or catastrophic. I felt at peace remembering all of the good the universe had bestowed upon me. These thoughts served as a reminder, too, that the universe was working to make everything *okay* with my son's addiction. Giving gratitude would somehow give me a sense of: *The universe is okay, I'm okay, and everything is working its way through as it's supposed to.*

Gratitude definitely helped pave the way for acceptance. The more gratitude I offered, the more blessings I counted, the more at peace I felt, and the more readily I was able to accept that everything unfolds as it should and all the worrying and stressing would not change that. I was able to accept that I was not in control. I didn't say I liked it, but at least I was able to gain that awareness and finally let go.

As I mentioned before, moms love to be in control. It's what we do best. We plan, we anticipate, we guide, we maneuver, we fix, we **handle it**. It's our full-time job as a mom. So, to be able to let go of a situation as serious as an addicted child is a huge undertaking. It honestly takes a leap of faith and an abundance of gratitude to be able to admit it's out of our control. But I can attest to the fact that *it's necessary*. Not only for your own wellbeing, but for your child's as well. Believe it or not. The more we try to control and manipulate the situation, the more fraught with worry and fear we become, the more consumed with fixing it we become, the less present we are for our child and for ourselves.

Once you begin to feel gratitude on a daily basis, and offer thanks several times a day, you will feel more at peace. With that peace comes the realization that we can't control everything in our child's life, not even a disease as serious as addiction, and we have to let go of trying to control it. We have to make a conscious effort to give this to the universe to take care of. And then with that realization comes the ability to think more calmly, see the situation more clearly, and accept it.

BEING PRESENT

All through this process you're becoming more *present.* Slowly but surely, you're regaining your sense of self. You're recapturing your ability to focus on more than just your child's addiction. You're more able to think of something other than his death. You're more alert, alive, and present for your family and yourself. You owe it to yourself to be present. You can't possibly take care of yourself if you're busy trying to control your child's addiction—an exercise in futility.

Sounds simple, I know. But it doesn't happen just like that. This takes work, it takes awareness, and it takes a concentrated effort on your part to put that *oxygen mask on first.* It will happen, but make the decision to put YOU first. Not only do your health and wellbeing and presence of mind deserve it, but your child, the addict, deserves and needs a mom who is present and healthy. Think about it. Does he need a mom who is falling apart, stressed out, making herself physically sick from worry and attempts to manage a circumstance that's out of her control? Don't kid yourself. Nobody needs nor wants that from their mom.

If your goal is to be there to support your child, a heroin addict, during his recovery, then now is the time to step up and get yourself well. If you want to be a pillar of strength and encouragement, then start now. If you want to be around to see your child fight his disease and work through it to be healthy again, then you need to make some changes now. And it all starts with *an attitude of gratitude.*

MOM'S NOT THE ONLY ONE

I wasn't the only one who learned gratitude throughout this journey. One day, post-rehab, while Dylan was living on the other side of the country, I checked in, as I did quite often, to see how he was doing. His response brought tears of pure joy to my eyes: "I love my life right now. I walked to work in the pouring rain today and still had a moment where I smiled to myself about how good life is."

Another time I texted him asking, "How you feeling?"

"Alive. Well. Grateful. Blessed. Fabulous," came the reply.

I saved that text and still look at it from time to time to remind myself how fortunate we really are. It still brings a smile to my face.

It takes time, it takes effort, but if you really look, there's *always* something to be grateful for. Sometimes it just takes the extreme darkness of a situation to show us the light.

*Please guide my thoughts and my words so that I may
continue to give gratitude for life's many blessings.
Grace me with the ability to see
the good in the world and
the many lessons that addiction
has brought to my family.
Please give me the strength and guidance
to take care of myself and
the ability to recognize all that the
universe provides for me
so that I can walk this journey with peace.
I ask this for my highest and greatest good.
And so it is.*

CHAPTER 15

FORGIVENESS - THE HIGHEST FORM OF LOVE

*In this journey called Life, we all have
the right to fully live and live fully.*

-Unknown

It would be remiss of me not to talk about forgiving. For a mom of a drug addicted child, there is so much to forgive.

SELF-FORGIVENESS

I had to begin with *myself.* Once I let go of the guilt, anger, and grief, I forgave myself for all the things I thought I did and did not do. I forgave myself for only knowing what I knew and only doing what I could do.

We moms do the best we can with a heart full of love for our addicted child. Remind yourself as often as you need to that *you didn't cause it and you cannot fix it.* Forgive yourself for anything you think you might have done "wrong." Only do what you can for your child—love him and support his recovery.

Forgiving ourselves is not easy at first. It takes time and patience, and a lot of soul searching. Sometimes, you just have to dig deep and practice good ole fashioned introspection.

Introspection gets its name from the Latin word *introspicere* which means to look inside. This is exactly what we moms have to learn to do. While we're busy looking out for everyone else and doing for everyone in the family, we barely have time to look at ourselves. We have to learn to examine our emotions and be self-aware of what we are feeling and why.

Taking some time to be still, be present, and willing to analyze what we're feeling and why we are doing what we're doing can help us begin to forgive ourselves. By looking inward, we become more self-aware. When we start to understand ourselves, our motives, and our behaviors, we can stop being so hard on ourselves. Loving ourselves is the first step to forgiveness.

LET GO AND FORGIVE

When you're ready, forgive your child, too. Let go of any resentments you might have towards him for the addiction he's battling. You might not even realize you have resentment, but if you look deep inside yourself, you might be surprised to find it's there. Remind yourself again, *you can hate the addiction without hating your child.* He's struggling with a disease. There's no reason for resentments. It's not about you. He did not choose to become an addict to hurt anyone.

While Dylan was in rehab, we both learned how important forgiveness is. His counselor had each of us make a list of things we wanted to ask the other forgiveness for. I hadn't even thought about it, but when I actually sat down and began to reflect on all the years of addictive behaviors we had survived, I realized I did have quite a list.

Some of the things I asked Dylan to forgive me for were: not being a perfect mom, enabling him, not talking to him sooner about his drug use, and being angry with him at times.

Dylan was able to let me know he had already forgiven me for these shortcomings.

When it was Dylan's turn, he asked me, "Mom, can you forgive me for bringing drugs into your home? Can you forgive me for not being a good role model for my brothers and sisters? Do you forgive me for all the hurt I've caused you?"

These were no brainers for me. I had forgiven my son all of these things and more before he even asked me to. I could forgive because I reminded myself often enough that the things Dylan did and said were not *him.* They were the addict in him.

The one question on his long list that gave me pause was, "Mom, can you forgive me for getting involved with drugs in the first place?" I had to stop and think about that one. I honestly wasn't sure I was ready to let that go yet.

I told Dylan, "I'm working on that one." After all the warnings and education about drug abuse he received while growing up, I felt some resentment that Dylan would even begin to explore the world of drugs. He knew better than that. And I had to admit, I was pissed.

But, as I reminded myself that this was *his journey,* I was finally able to forgive him for starting to use drugs and launching himself on the path to addiction. For whatever reason, everything had happened the way it was supposed to, including his drug use. Who am I to judge his path? I had no reason *not* to forgive my son.

ULTIMATE LOVE

Forgiveness is freeing; it's cleansing; it's energizing, and it left my heart open for only love. I know that my forgiveness helped Dylan as much as his forgiveness allowed me to let go of any negative feelings I was holding on to. Forgiveness is a necessity for the soul.

But when your son is addicted to drugs, forgiving doesn't stop with him. I learned to forgive the people I felt didn't do *enough* to help Dylan. I forgave the people who did nothing at all and distanced themselves from him. I forgave the folks who judged our family from afar. It serves no purpose to hold on to negativity, resentments, and hurt caused by other people. The only person suffering was *me*. So, I learned forgiveness and haven't had a moment of regret since. I chose forgiveness for **me.** Life is far too fleeting to dwell on negative emotions.

Make your list of those things you'd like to forgive others for as well as those you need to forgive yourself for. Then work on each one. It takes time, patience, some soul-searching, and a lot of love. But you will learn to let everything else go. You'll feel the positive changes happening in your life once you begin to forgive.

Remember that self-forgiveness is as important as forgiving others. You've beat yourself up long enough for your son's battle with addiction. Forgive and, most of all, love yourself.

*Allow me to forgive myself for
anything I may have done
or not done for my addicted child.
Teach me to forgive and love myself again.
Help me to forgive my son for the
things he has said and done
that hurt me during his addiction.
Remind me that my son and the
addict are not the same person.
Give me the love and strength to
forgive those who hurt my son
and our family through their words or actions
while he struggled with addiction.
Help me to feel only compassion towards them.
I ask this for my highest and greatest good.
And so it is.*

POSTSCRIPT
BREATHE—THE JOURNEY
CONTINUES

I thought I had finally finished my first book. It had taken me a couple of years, on and off, in between the kids, the house, the job, and 1,000 other things, but there I was, getting ready to put the finishing touches on my labor of love.

Dylan was still living and working in California and working on his recovery (as far as I knew). And then the cell phone dinged.

I thought it must be Dylan with a "Happy Easter" text from California to say he would call later in the day. It was him. I was right about that. But he was texting with an apology. "Mom, I'm so sorry for ruining your Easter. And your life."

I was too shocked to respond at first as he continued to inform me he had relapsed and was surviving day to day in a motel room.

The ironic part? At the time I received his text, I was on the couch reading a new book I had just picked up about addiction. As I read it, I realized, any one of us moms could have written that book. The families, the stories, the behaviors, the excuses, the hopes, the devastation are all the same. And now I was faced with the next chapter in our own story.

I won't pretend my heart didn't sink or that I didn't cry and feel that familiar sudden rush of despair grip my chest. But I will admit that something had changed. Not my love, or my caring. But I didn't have the sudden urgency to fix it this time. My reaction wasn't to jump in and help, even though that is exactly what Dylan was asking me to do.

Instead, I prayed. Oh, and I also told him how upset I was that he relapsed and had lied to me about it. I get it, temptation comes with addiction. It doesn't mean relapse has to. (Although, I am quite aware and understand that relapse does often come with the road to recovery. I was just tired of that word by this point.) Where's the tools he had learned in rehab? Where's the strength, the willingness, and the power to fight this? I wasn't seeing any of it. I couldn't fix it, and no, I couldn't help. All I could do was pray and keep hope that my son would figure this out on his own and turn the corner to his final destination of recovery.

Fast forward a few weeks. My son, the heroin addict, jobless and homeless, was on a plane from California to New York to return to the family who loves and supports him. (He missed his original flight because he had passed out during the boarding process happening around him.)

Now he would be home. Maybe I could talk some sense into him. Make him return to rehab. Make him smarten up!

Reality check – again! At this point in his journey, Dylan wanted no part of another rehab. He had himself convinced, as addicts sometimes do, he didn't need it. "I can do this on my own. I don't need rehab. I won't go again."

I reminded him often, "You can't do this alone, Dylan. You need treatment. You need support." The debate went on for a week or more with no progress as far as I could see. He refused treatment. And his mind wasn't changing. He did attend AA and NA meetings and tried the best way he knew to *stay clean*. He stayed in the house, isolating himself from the outside perils and pitfalls. He stuck close to his family, spending his time with his siblings or myself. We all knew he wasn't ready to look for work or see anyone he once knew. So, I waited, I watched, I hovered, I protected, and I prayed.

I've watched my son go through withdrawal before. It's never pretty, and it's not something a mother wants to experience. But it's part of living with an addicted child. This would not be the first time Dylan believed he had the strength to conquer his addiction if he "could just get through the withdrawal."

So, Mom stayed home and kept a vigilant eye on her son withdrawing from opiates. It still hurts my heart to think of what Dylan went through. The chills, the pain, the intense nausea, the restless legs, the vomiting, the body aches, the anxiety. There isn't much a mother can do but stand by and watch, and pray. When he was able to sleep, I would watch him and ask myself yet again *How did we get here?*

Within several days, Dylan was feeling better. He made it through his own abbreviated method of "detox." Although I was grateful and relieved, I knew this was only the beginning. I knew all too well that the real battle had just began.

Each day that went by, Dylan felt a little better. He was more active and more talkative. I encouraged him, I praised him, I thanked him, I tried to keep him busy, and I helped him keep hope. He was using some of the tools he had learned in rehab to keep his recovery moving forward, but it was evident that he was struggling with his new-found sobriety. There were still the cravings, the triggers, not to mention the adjustment of living a clean life again.

For anyone watching from afar, it would probably seem effortless. For an addict (and a mom who's been here before with her son), effort was merely the tip of this iceberg. It was going to take much more than just effort. There would be a whole lot of self-love, forgiveness, strength, support, understanding, honesty, coping skills, strategies, and communication needed—just to name a few.

Dylan was clean and sober about two weeks. He worked hard for those two weeks doing everything he could to focus on his recovery. One evening I watched him physically struggling. He was quiet, seemed to be slipping into a depression, and it was an exceptionally bad day for his anxiety. His leg bounced as it always did when he was anxious. I made sure to stay close by in case he needed anything. He wasn't in the mood for conversation and continuously assured me he was "doing okay." I had a bad feeling though.

As I sat with him in the living room, I received a text out of the blue from my friend, Maria, who asked how Dylan was doing. She knew he had relapsed and was home from California. I kept my answer brief: "He's not doing too good. I'll talk to you tomorrow." This particular friend is part of our local recovery team. She asked if she could come by "just to talk." I answered, "Not tonight. Maybe tomorrow." I knew Dylan was not in the mood for talking, and I didn't feel like seeing anyone. I was more concerned with keeping a vigilant watch over my son to help him over this bump.

Maria would not take "no" for an answer. She insisted, "I can be there in ten minutes. Maybe it would help to just talk. Just give me the okay." I insisted it wasn't a good time, and said, "let's talk tomorrow." But then, something told me to give in when her next text read, "I'm only a few minutes away. I'll grab another Recovery Team Member and we'll be right over." Somehow, Maria had sensed there was an urgency. And, again, the universe stepped in on our behalf.

I didn't say anything to Dylan yet. As I left the room to tell his father they were coming over to talk to us, Dylan got up and went to the bathroom.

As promised, ten minutes later, Maria and Chris, both recovery team "angels," came through the door. This was just about the same time I realized that Dylan was still in the bathroom—and it had been an unusually long time. My heart dropped as I knocked on the bathroom door. He walked out and saw our guests, and I introduced them, explaining they wanted to "just talk" to him. He sat down on the sofa, and I knew immediately what had taken him so long in the bathroom. His demeanor told me all I needed to know. The anxiety and uncomfortableness of the past week and a half was too much for him. So, Dylan did what he knew would relieve his stress immediately. He used heroin.

He didn't deny it when asked. All he could say was, "I'm sorry." My heart was broken for him. I knew he was trying so hard to stay clean and sober. I also saw how difficult it was for him and knew he needed professional help. But he had refused. So, I figured this was good timing. The professionals were with him and they would know what to say to him. We left them alone with Dylan while I silently prayed they would talk him into going to rehab.

Only a few minutes passed. Suddenly, I heard Maria shout, "Do you have a Narcan kit? Grab it! Quick!"

As I tried to process what was happening, Chris yelled, "He's dropping, grab the Narcan out of my car! Now!"

Narcan is Naloxone, a prescribed medication, in a nasal spray that's used to counteract an opioid overdose. Yes, *overdose.* I had taken the training months earlier and had a kit with me at all times. Although a mother never really believes she will ever have to use Narcan, I was never without it nearby. Just in case.

As I ran to get the Narcan, my mind tried to adjust to what was happening. I remember thinking, *this can't really be happening. It's a bad dream. I am not going to watch my son die.*

From the other room, I could hear Chris yelling Dylan's name and slapping his cheek and legs to get him to wake up. *Please let him wake up!*

I found the Narcan kit and ran as fast as my legs would carry me back to the living room. Just at that moment, Dylan opened his eyes ever so slightly. Quick thinking as he was, Chris immediately grabbed him and hoisted him up under his arms to a standing position. *Or was Chris actually holding him upright?* He wasted no time getting Dylan on his own two feet and walking, although just barely. Chris instantly whisked Dylan outside into the brisk night air.

I was frozen with fear and shock and just stood there watching this scene play out while my mind kept repeating, *I cannot believe this is happening.* I watched as Dylan slowly came around and was finally able to put some coherent words together. Again, his first thought was to apologize.

Flooded with relief, I had to leave the room while I sobbed tears of gratitude that he wasn't dead. By now, I knew all too well that often overdose is a part of addiction. Too frequently recently we would hear of another young person in our community who lost their battle with addiction through an overdose. And every time, whether I knew the person or not, my heart broke a little more. With each overdose, my anger rose and I would think, how *pointless* and *avoidable* such a death is! *It just shouldn't happen!*

I also understood how fortunate we were that this recovery team had been present at exactly the right moment in Dylan's journey. Once again, his life had been spared. And at that moment, I made a mental addition to the top of my Gratitude List.

Maria and Chris spent time with Dylan, talking to him, listening to him. They said all the right things and listened with compassion as he steadfastly told them, "I'm not going to rehab again. I can't do it. I'll get clean on my own."

The discussion lasted for a couple of hours with little progress as far as I could tell. But, eventually, Dylan capitulated just enough to promise he would go to detox in the morning. The plan was made for the recovery team to return the following day to pick him up and drive him to a detox facility. It was everyone's hope that Dylan would agree to go to rehab from there once he was thinking a little clearer.

Just possibly, this was one of the longest nights of my life. Dylan stretched out on one sofa while I lay on the other and watched him sleep all night. And I prayed, *let him choose to go to rehab. Let him start his recovery. Help him to be clean and sober again.*

Morning came. Dylan awoke. And the debate began. He wasn't going to detox willingly, and I didn't see any other option. We went back and forth for a couple of hours on the subject.

Finally, Dylan relented: "Alright, I'll go to detox. But I am not going to rehab." I figured we would cross that bridge when we got to it, and in the meantime, I would take what I could get.

Detox was a great start.

A couple of hours later, I kissed him goodbye. Again. As I watched him walk down the hospital corridor, I prayed that this would be the last time I had to say goodbye to my son. I was relieved he was safe and getting treatment but my heart was heavy knowing that this time was different. This seemed more of a struggle than the other times. This time he was fighting treatment and he had never done that before. All I could do was hope.

Four long days later, Dylan called. "I'm finished with detox. I'm coming home."

Even though he had warned me of his intentions, I was still shocked. I'd made myself believe he would see what was best.

"What are you talking about? You just got there!" I tried to talk him into going to rehab.

"I'm not going to rehab. The people here already tried to convince me to go. They told me I'm stupid for not going. But I'm coming home."

I know I could have said "no." But instead, I picked him up a few hours later and brought my son home.

FAST FORWARD

As this book goes to print, Dylan is living at home, working part-time while back in college full-time, and working on his recovery on his own, in his own way. He now has over a year in recovery and his incredible sense of humor back. He has reconnected with his siblings and has a new set of positive people he calls friends. I watch as he slowly transforms himself into the person he wants to be. He reflects on his journey. He doesn't pretend it never happened. He doesn't judge others, and he doesn't spend time with others who do.

There are so many moments I look at him and smile as I think, *how far we've come, how fortunate we are, and what a beautiful soul he truly is.* It would be easy to forget the horrors he's overcome.

But I still remind myself *this is his journey. There's bound to be bumps, but he has to walk his own path. I will not try to control it. The only thing I am in control of is my own behavior.* I can only pray for and look forward to the day when I no longer carry that Narcan kit wherever I go.

And Dylan lovingly reminds me once in a while, "An addict is always an addict, Mom." That doesn't mean he is actively using drugs. What it does mean is addiction is lifelong. It will always be there for him. There is no cure but there is recovery. Addiction is always a work in progress with daily reminders and triggers and even cravings sometimes. Fortunately, recovery is always a daily process, too, with coping strategies, support, and many valuable tools.

Although I understand what those in the world of addiction mean by "an addict is always an addict" I have my own opinion on the subject. I don't call Dylan an addict anymore. I prefer to call him my amazing, loving, smart, compassionate, son who has been to hell and back. I prefer to focus on the beautiful life he is living in the present moment rather than reliving the past or stressing about what the future holds. I choose to remain positive and know that the universe is watching out for him. Addiction doesn't define my son nor is "addict" his title.

My daily prayers and mantras still get me through every day with a brighter outlook. I ask the universe several times a day to help Dylan maintain his sobriety and his happiness. (Yes, I say it out loud because I know the universe is listening!)

I don't take any of this journey for granted, and I have tried my best not to miss the lessons it brought. Although I won't ever forget what we have been through, I also don't dwell on it. Every day is a gift, and I adore presents! Who doesn't? So, I accept them graciously and do my part to make the most of every day that has been given to us.

My mother's intuition screams, *there could be more to come!* but my mother's heart holds on to gratitude, love, and most of all, hope. In the meantime, all we can do is *keep on keepin' on.* The alternative is not an option.

"You can't go back and change the beginning
but you can start where you are
and change the ending."
--C.S. Lewis

LETTER TO MOTHERS OF HEROIN ADDICTS

Dear mom of a heroin addict,

Thank you for everything you have done to help your addicted child. Thank you for being the constant in the equation, the calm in the storm, the stability in the upheaval of a tormented life.

You are an amazing woman and a special person. You were there through it all, and you endured more sadness and pain than any woman should feel in her lifetime.

Thank you for never giving up, walking away, or turning your back.

Thank you for getting out of bed in the morning when it would have been easier to hide under the covers knowing what the day would bring.

Thank you for doing everything in your power to help your addicted child, for supporting him, and most of all, for loving him.

Thank you for ignoring the comments and criticisms from family, friends, and even strangers who felt they knew better and tried to tell you how to handle it.

Thank you for going above and beyond what the professionals told you to do and trusting your intuition, your gut, when you knew something wasn't right.

Thank you for always supporting your addicted child on the good days and the very low days.

Thank you for having the strength to push through the chaos and holding your head up when you went out into the world every day.

Thank you for praying for him while crying in your pillow at night instead of losing it in front of the entire family.

Thank you, Mom, for stepping up, for showing up, and for being you.

You were given a rough road to traverse but everything you did and are doing for your addicted child is helping to change this world every day. Never doubt for a minute that someone is watching, someone is learning from your example. Don't doubt that what you're doing is for the best.

For whatever reason, your child was given a difficult journey, and you have been there with him along the path to support, love, and encourage.

Thank you for being a light in the world, for doing everything in your power to change it, and for handling the challenges with grace and love.

Thank you for just being a MOM.

With love and admiration,

All the moms with a child addicted to heroin

MANY THANKS

My sincere gratitude for all the people who supported my journey as I wrote this book.

To the friends and family who coaxed, encouraged me, and were there for me through the years and the tears. You know who you are. I love you all.

To all of the experts at Author Academy Elite for their unending guidance and patience.

To my cover designer, Yesna99 at 99designs.com.

To Vanessa, whose red pen and friendship have blessed me.

To the moms who came before me and offered love and support.

To Sierra, Dylan, Jensen, Trey, and Sage, my beacons of light.

To my own beautiful mom who gifted me with her strength and resilience.

And to my Angels and the Universe for the guidance and countless blessings.

I am eternally grateful.

ABOUT THE AUTHOR

Lynn Hotaling is a blessed mother of five living in upstate New York. She holds degrees in Psychology and Chemical Dependency Counseling and is a Certified Reiki Practitioner. She has experience working, volunteering, and researching in the field of addictions treatment.

Made in the USA
Columbia, SC
27 April 2023

15870900R00120